Library of Congress Cataloging-in-Publication Data
Gates, Henry Louis.
Loose canons: notes on the culture wars / Henry Louis Gates, Jr.
p.   cm.   Includes index.
ISBN 0-19-507519-9

Printed in the United States of America
on acid-free paper

Text Acknowledgments

The following essays in this collection have been previously published:

"Canon Confidential" first appeared in the *New York Times Book Review*, 1990.

"The Master's Pieces" first appeared in the *South Atlantic Quarterly* in 1990.

"Writing, 'Race,' and the Difference It Makes" first appeared in *Critical Inquiry* in 1985.

"Talking Black" was given as a talk at a Modern Language Association panel, "Integrity and the Black Tradition," and first appeared in the *Voice Literary Supplement* in 1988.

"'Tell Me, Sir, . . . What *Is* "Black" Literature?'" first appeared in *PMLA* in 1990.

"African-American Studies in the 21st Century" first appeared in a slightly different form in *Newsweek* in 1991.

"'What's in a Name?'" first appeared in *Dissent* in Fall 1989.

"Trading on the Margin" was delivered as part of a symposium on canon formation at the American Studies Association in 1990, and first appeared in *American Literary History* in 1991.

Contents

Introduction   xi

I   LITERATURE

1 / Canon Confidential: A Sam Slade Caper   3

2 / The Master's Pieces: On Canon Formation and
the African-American Tradition   17

3 / Writing, "Race," and the Difference
It Makes   43

4 / Talking Black: Critical Signs of the Times   71

II   THE PROFESSION

5 / "Tell Me, Sir, . . . What *Is*
'Black' Literature?"   87

6 / Integrating the American Mind   105

7 / African-American Studies in the
21st Century   121

III   SOCIETY

8 / "What's in a Name?" Some Meanings of
Blackness   131

9 / The Big Picture   153

10 / Trading on the Margin: Notes on the Culture
of Criticism   173

Index   195

Introduction

Few commentators could have predicted that one of the issues dominating academic and popular discourse in the final decade of the twentieth century — concomitant with the fall of apartheid in South Africa, communism in Russia, and the subsequent dissolution of the Soviet Union — would be the matter of cultural pluralism in our high school and college curricula and its relation to the "American" national identity. Stories on race and education have appeared on the covers of *Time, Newsweek,* and *U.S. News and World Report;* in television news magazines such as "The MacNeil-Lehrer Report" and William Buckley's "Firing Line"; and in hundreds of news items in the daily press — attesting to the urgency of the scattered, and often confused, debates over what is variously known as cultural diversity, cultural pluralism, or multiculturalism. And not only are these matters pressing in this country: In September 1991, the *New York Times* could note that "East and West agreed today — the greatest threat to civil liberties was no longer communism, but violent nationalistic passions unleashed by its collapse."

Increasing incidents of violence are associated with ethnic differences in very many places in the world: Hasidim and African-Americans in Crown Heights, Brooklyn; Serbs and Croats in Yugoslavia; Koreans and African-Americans in Flatbush, Brooklyn; Zulus and Xhosas in South Africa; Poles and Gypsies in Poland; the Tutsis and Hutu in Rwanda; the Yoruba and Igbos in Nigeria; and, of course, the fate of the Jews in Ethiopia and in the Soviet Union. The list seems to grow longer, rather than shorter, as we stumble our way as a society into the twenty-first century. In 1903, W.E.B. Du Bois could write, prophetically, that the problem of the twentieth century would be the color line. We might well argue that the problem of the twenty-first century will be the problem of ethnic differences, as these conspire with complex differences in color, gender, and class. As actual cultural differences between social and ethnic groups are being brought to bear to justify the subordination of one group by another, the matter of multiculturalism becomes politically fraught. Until these differences are understood in an era of emergent nationalism, the challenge of mutual understanding among the world's multifarious cultures will be the single greatest task that we face, after the failure of the world to feed itself.

The essays collected here are the attempts of a critic of literature and culture to examine the implications of nationalistic eruptions and the politics of identity for the future of American society and culture, for our university and public school curricula, and, to be sure, for literary and cultural studies themselves. Perhaps it should seem anomalous that I, a person whose first scholarly passion is the recovery and editing of "lost" and ignored texts, should find myself preoccupied with these questions. And yet, what is often referred to loosely as the "multicultural" movement traces its origins in the academy to the birth of Afro-American Studies in the late 1960s.

Just as the birth of black studies had both a larger social as well as an academic dimension, so, too, have recent academic debates about the curriculum and America's ever-increasing proliferation of subcultures. That literary scholars and their works have been assigned central roles in the public drama of cultural pluralism and its place in our schools — that is, that members of Congress, governors and their staffs, and even President Bush find it necessary to enter the debate about the nature and function of our curriculum and what its shape (and perhaps, colors) shall be in the next century — is one of the more curious developments in the recent social history of this country.

When, to put the matter bluntly, have literary studies so engaged the attention of American society at large? Why does William F. Buckley take the time to inveigh against Stanley Fish and Catherine Stimpson on "Firing Line," when a decade ago Mr. Buckley would have found the idea of inviting two literary theorists to his studios most improbable? Particularly following two decades of what was once called *high theory*, replete with difficult ideas enveloped in equally difficult jargon, the apparent social and political "relevance" of the thinking of literary scholars to the actual lives of our fellow citizens is quite astonishing. For a scholar of African-American Studies, this new state of affairs is especially gratifying, given the link between the social and economic conditions of African-Americans and our field of inquiry. Debates about multiculturalism have given to literary studies a renewed urgency.

But is the political and social significance of our work as immediate as all that? Or is the noisy spectacle of the public debate a kind of stage behind which far narrower gains are secured or relinquished? I must confess to considerable ambivalence on the matter. The "larger issues" that frame the classroom clamor are profoundly real: but the significance of our own interventions is easily over-stated; and I do not exempt myself from this admonition.

To both its proponents and its antagonists, multi-culturalism represents—either refreshingly or frighten-ingly—a radical departure. Like most claims of cultural novelty, this one is more than a little exaggerated. For both the challenge of cultural pluralism and the varied forms of political resistance to it go back to the founding of our republic.

In the university today, it must be admitted, the chal-lenge has taken on a peculiar inflection. But the underly-ing questions are time-tested. What does it mean to be an American? Must academic inquiry be subordinated to the requirements of national identity? Should scholarship and education reflect our actual diversity, or should they, rather, forge a communal identity that may not yet have been achieved?

For answers, you can, of course, turn to the latest jeremiad on the subject from, say, George Will, Dinesh D'Sousa, or Roger Kimball. But in fact, these questions have always occasioned lively disagreement among American educators. In 1917, William Henry Hulme de-cried "the insidious introduction into our scholarly rela-tions of the political propaganda of a wholly narrow, selfish, and vicious nationalism and false patriotism." His opponents were equally emphatic in their beliefs. "More and more clearly," Fred Lewis Pattee ventured in 1919, "is it seen now that the American soul, the American conception of democracy, Americanism should be made prominent in our school curriculums, as a guard against the rising spirit of experimental lawlessness." Sound fa-miliar?

Given the political nature of the debate over educa-tion and the national interest, the conservative penchant of charging the multiculturalists with "politics" is a little perplexing. For conservative critics, to their credit, have never hesitated to provide a political defense of what they consider the "traditional" curriculum: The future of the republic, they argue, depends on the inculcation of proper civic virtues. What these virtues are is a matter of vehement dispute. But to speak of a curriculum untouched by political concerns is to imagine — as no one does — that education could take place in a vacuum.

Stated simply, the thrust of the pieces gathered here is this: Ours is a late-twentieth-century world profoundly fissured by nationality, ethnicity, race, class, and gender. And the only way to transcend those divisions — to forge, for once, a civic culture that respects both differences and commonalities — is through education that seeks to comprehend the diversity of human culture. Beyond the hype and the high-flown rhetoric is a pretty homely truth: There is no tolerance without respect — and no respect without knowledge. Any human being sufficiently curious and motivated can fully possess another culture, no matter how "alien" it may appear to be.

Indeed, the historical architects of the university always understood this. As Cardinal Newman wrote over a century ago, the university should promote "the power of viewing many things at once as one whole, referring them severally to their true place in the universal system, of understanding their respective values, and determining their mutual dependence." In just this vein, the critic Edward Said has recently suggested that "Our model for academic freedom should therefore be the migrant or traveler: for if, in the real world outside the academy, we must needs be ourselves and only ourselves, inside the academy we should be able to discover and travel among other selves, other identities, other varieties of the human adventure. But most essentially, in this joint discovery of self and other, it is the role of the academy to transform what might be conflict, or context, or assertion into reconciliation, mutuality, recognition, creative interaction."

But if multiculturalism represents the culmination of an age-old ideal—the dream known, in the seventeenth century, as *mathesis universalis*—why has it been the target of such ferocious attacks?

The conservative desire has been to cast the debate in terms of the West versus the Rest. And yet that's the very opposition that the pluralist wants to challenge. Pluralism sees culture as porous, dynamic, and interactive, rather than as the fixed property of particular ethnic groups. Thus the idea of a monolithic, homogeneous "West" itself comes into question (nothing new here: literary historians have pointed out that the very concept of "Western culture" may date back only to the eighteenth century). But rather than mourning the loss of some putative ancestral purity, we can recognize what's valuable, resilient, even cohesive in the hybrid and variegated nature of our modernity.

Cultural pluralism is not, of course, everyone's cup of tea. Vulgar cultural nationalists—like Allan Bloom or Leonard Jeffries—correctly identify it as the enemy. These polemicists thrive on absolute partitions: between "civilization" and "barbarism," between "black" and "white," between a thousand versions of Us and Them. But they are whistling in the wind.

For whatever the outcome of the culture wars in the academy, the world we live in is multicultural already. Mixing and hybridity are the rule, not the exception. As a student of African-American culture, of course, I've come to take this kind of cultural palimpsest for granted. Duke Ellington, Miles Davis, and John Coltrane have influenced popular musicians the world over. Wynton Marsalis is as comfortable with Mozart as with jazz. Anthony Davis writes in a musical idiom that combines Bartok with the blues. In the dance, Judith Jameson, Alvin Ailey, and Katherine Dunham all excelled at "Western" cultural forms, melding these with African-American styles to produce performances that were neither, and both. In painting, Romare Bearden and Jacob Lawrence, Martin Puryear and Augusta Savage, learned to paint and sculpt by studying Western artists, yet each has pioneered the construction of a distinctly African-American visual art. And in literature, of course, the most formally complex and compelling black writers—such as Jean Toomer, Sterling Brown, Langston Hughes, Zora Hurston, Richard Wright, Ralph Ellison, James Baldwin, Toni Morrison, and Gwendolyn Brooks—have always blended forms of Western literature with African-American vernacular and written traditions. Then again, even a vernacular form like the spirituals took as its texts the King James version of the Old and New Testaments. Morrison's master's thesis was on Virginia Woolf and Faulkner; Rita Dove is as conversant with German literature as she is with that of her own country. African-American culture, then, has been a model of multiculturalism and plurality. And it is this cultural impulse, I believe, that represents the very best hope for us, collectively, to forge a new, and vital, common American culture in the twenty-first century.

With just a few exceptions, the pieces collected here orginated as talks prepared for oral delivery, and have been altered very little since. All bear the impress of the occasion that produced them. In particular: "The Master's Pieces" was originally given at a conference on cultural diversity at Duke University in 1988. "Talking Black" in part originated as a Modern Language Association panel discussion, "Integrity and the Black Tradition." (A bit of context: "theory" was, at the time, frequently depicted as inimical to the supposed communal trust of black nationalism, an opposition I sought to undermine.) "Integrating the American Mind" was first given as a talk to the New Jersey State Superintendents of Education in 1987, an audience mostly composed of state college administrators. "African-American Studies in the 21st Century" was a talk given at the 1991 Wisconsin Conference on African-American Studies; and "Trading on the Margin" (originally entitled "Good-bye, Columbus?") was a talk given at a panel, "Firing the Canon" at the 1990 American Studies Association. The collection of these talks and essays must be credited to Elizabeth Maguire, my splendid editor at Oxford University Press, who persevered, despite an at times foot-dragging author, in the belief that these briefs, however occasional, might have somewhat more than ephemeral interest, and who organized and edited them into something very much like a book.

Now, I should admit up front that there are significant differences in perspective and emphasis among these pieces. Some of them speak with a confidence greater than I now can muster. Some strike me as insufficiently critical, others as excessively critical: with hindsight, I fear I have sometimes been in the hapless position of blowing up balloons and then pricking them. I realize, as well, that guild speeches, addressed to members of my profession, can trail clouds of stale cigarette smoke in a manner offputting to those who are outside these institutions, and those who imagine themselves to be. Then again, one of my concerns is to take a stand against the delightful if reflexive rhetoric of institution bashing, a rhetoric that is itself highly institutionalized.

Even so, I feel pangs of misgiving when I look over this collection, since it records, in a sense, what I was doing when I wasn't doing what I was supposed to be doing. Literary criticism and scholarship are discussed here, but not practiced. But that, too, is symptomatic of these past few years of foment, dissension, and position taking, of a time in which audiences, both general and academic, were much more interested in my position in the contemporary "culture wars" than in my analysis of

nineteenth-century slave narratives. Nor do I think we
have safely emerged from the other end. Today, the
mindless celebration of difference for its own sake is no
more tenable than the nostalgic return to some mono-
chrome homogeneity. My hope is to have contributed,
however stumblingly, to the search for a middle way.

Cambridge, Massachusetts   H.L.G., jr
September 1991

I

LITERATURE

CHAPTER
1

Canon Confidential: A Sam Slade Caper

Her name was Estelle. I should have known the broad spelled trouble when she came into my office and started talking about the canon. The literary canon.

I stubbed out my Lucky Strike and glanced up at her, taking in her brass-blond hair, all curled and stiff with spray. Like she had a still of Betty Grable taped to the corner of her mirror.

Turned out she'd been peddling her story for the past couple of years. Nobody would take it on; I shouldn't have either. But when I was a kid I used to write doggerel. Maybe that's why I didn't throw the babe out of my office.

"Tell me what I need to know, sugar." I splashed some bourbon in my coffee mug, put my feet on my desk, and listened.

Seemed there was some kind of a setup that determined which authors get on this A list of great literature. Payout was all perks, so far as I could make out. If you're on this list, they teach your work in school and write

3

critical essays on you. Waldenbooks moves you from the Fiction section to the Literature section. I couldn't figure where the percentage was, unless some big shot was getting a cut of the reprint royalties, but she didn't think that was it.

"So what are you saying? You want me to shut down this operation? Round up the bad guys?"

"Nothing like that," she said huskily. "I got no beef with the canon as such. It serves a legit purpose." She looked around nervously and lowered her voice. "What I'm telling you is, it's fixed. It's not on the level." She paused. "What I'm telling you is, this is the biggest scam since the 1919 World Series."

I whistled softly. "We're talking thousands of books, right? The jewels of Western culture, right?"

She nodded. "You'll be going up against the big boys. Does that scare you?"

I patted my shoulder holster. "I'm prepared."

"You get twenty-five a day plus expenses," she said.

I said, "Fair enough." It was all Philip Marlowe got in *Trouble is My Business.*

■ ■ ■

The first person I spoke to was Helen Vendler, and all she was sure of was I was wasting my time.

I found her at the Harvard Club, on Forty-fourth Street off Fifth Avenue, eating alone. She swore up and down I was being snookered.

"Oh, I hear the talk. But it's just a tabloid fantasy," she assured me, fastidiously squeezing a lemon section over her oysters. "There is no overlord, Slade. Nobody's fixing what we read — the whole idea's preposterous. If a book's good, people read it. If it's bad, people won't."

She was smug about it. Too smug.

"They've got something on you, don't they?" I said, thinking hard. "That's why they let you edit *The Harvard*

Book of Contemporary American Poetry—because they knew you'd do their dirty work for them."

She wasn't smiling anymore. "You won't get a thing out of me," she said. Then I saw her make eye contact with the bouncer. All three hundred pounds of him. "Malloy," she said quietly, "get him out of here."

Figured a walk would do me good anyway.

I looked up a few of the writers I knew, but I didn't fare much better. It was like somebody had gotten to them first. Harold Brodkey told me he'd like to talk about it, only he'd grown too fond of his kneecaps. Toni Morrison was hiding out in Key West. And Cynthia Ozick slammed her front door on my thumb.

I was making the rounds at Columbia when a black Cadillac with tinted windows pulled up alongside me on Broadway at 115th Street. Two pugs came out and threw me in the back seat like a sack of potatoes.

"Let me be blunt, Mr. Slade. Do you know what happens to people who stick their noses into other people's business?"

On my left, Elizabeth Hardwick. On my right, one of her gorillas. I turned to the lady.

"I seen *Chinatown*," I murmured.

"A good film," she said. "But not a great one. The great ones are those taught in film classes, in universities around the country. For example, anything by Eisenstein."

"I saw one of his films once. Bored me stiff."

"As it does avid film students around the world. But that, my friend, is how canonization works. All the films you'd never see if it were up to you, all the books you'd never read if you really had a choice—they are the very lifeblood of the canon."

"You're losing me, Lizzy."

"Come, come. The nineteenth-century American novels that go on for hundreds of mind-numbing pages about cetaceans. The endless Russian novels about theodicy, suffering, and salvation, with an unpronounceable cast of thousands. Where would they be without the required reading list?"

"Out of print?" I hazarded.

"You see why we can't let you continue, then." She patted my knee consolingly. "There's simply too much at stake."

The car probably wasn't going much more than twenty miles an hour when they threw me out.

Fact was, I didn't much like being manhandled by literary mandarins. But now I had a pretty good hunch about where to look next.

I caught up with Alfred Kazin in the New York Public Library; I figured he had to know something. Maybe he did, but when I mentioned the canon, he turned nasty.

"Beat it," he growled. "I've got nothing to say to you."

I grabbed him by the collar, lifted him a few inches off the floor, and brought his face real close to mine. "Are we having a communication problem?"

"Please," he murmured, his head lolling against Edmund Wilson's *Letters on Literature and Politics*. "You know I don't make the decisions."

"I've heard that tune more often than Pachelbel's Canon. Don't sweet-talk me, punk. Who's in on it?"

His eyes glinted. "Look, it's an institutional configuration. It's societal. *Everybody*'s in on it."

"Oh, get off it," I snapped. "Try telling that to the gals who never made it into the great American procession. Try telling that to Phillis Wheatley. Or Zora Neale Hurston. Or Charlotte Perkins Gilman." I poked him in the chest. "You guys really did a job on them. Kept them out in the cold."

"You still mad about that?" He rolled his eyes. "Hell, we made it up to them. Everybody's reading those broads

today. Take a look at any freshman syllabus; they're practically compulsory." He mopped the sweat off his brow.
"Look, better late than never, right?"

"That's not the point and you know it. Now tell me
who supplies you."

His eyes darted around the stacks, and then he loos-
ened up. That's when I knew something was wrong.

"I believe the person you want is right behind you,"
he smirked.

Something hard jabbed into my back.

I turned around slowly, my hands held high.

It was Jacques Barzun, a .38 Beretta resting comfortably in one hand. He was in black tie, looking like he'd
just stepped out of a cocktail party.

"Big surprise," I said, trying to look more relaxed than
I was. "Shoulda figured this one out myself."

"There are a great many things you should have figured out, Mr. Slade."

"Yeah? Gimme a for instance."

"Standards, Mr. Slade. Do you know what standards
are?" His menacing smile was perfect—probably practiced it in front of a mirror.

"No culture without norms, Mr. Slade. It's an elementary principle. History gives us no reason for optimism
about the triumph of civilization over barbarity. Where
we do not move forward, we regress. To be sure, it begins
with slight lapses. Errors of usage— confusing *disinterest*
with *uninterest,* using *hopefully* for *it is to be hoped.* And
then, with astonishing swiftness, the rot sets in. With our
sense of language dulled, who can appreciate the exqui-
site verbal precision of the very finest literature? We cease
to judge, we join the relativist's party of mindless tolerance, we descend into the torpor of cultural egalitari-
anism."

"Sounds ugly," I said.

"It is."

"Even so," I said levelly, "you wouldn't shoot me."

"Wouldn't I?" He raised an eyebrow.

"You don't have a silencer," I pointed out, "and the sign says to be quiet in the library."

I knew I had him there.

■ ■ ■

There was one more lead I had to check out. Word on the street had it that a certain Harold Bloom was deeply involved in the whole business. He was a critic who taught at Yale and moonlighted at City College. I figured the time might be right to pay him a visit. I didn't talk conspiracy with him. Just said people around town thought he knew a lot about canon formation. Maybe even had something to do with it himself.

Bloom folded his hands together under his chin. "My dear, the strong poet will abide. The weak will not. All else is commentary. Politics has nothing to do with it."

Something else was bothering me, and I decided to be up-front. "I noticed the cops paid you a visit before I came by. What'd they want?"

"I'm a suspect, if you can believe it." He looked at me wide-eyed. "Somebody killed off Thomas Stearns Eliot, and they think I had something to do with it. Imagine that. Little old me." Then he grinned, and I saw he could be a very dangerous man.

So Tommy was dead. That should have cheered me up, but it didn't. From a pay phone on the corner, I made a quick call to an old friend in the NYPD. Turned out Bloom had a rap sheet longer than a three-part *New Yorker* profile. They were after him for a whole series of murders, from Matthew Arnold to Robert Lowell. All of them savaged with bloody dispatch, often in a paragraph or less. So far, they couldn't pin anything on him.

The police were biding their time. Seems they had a decoy all set up. A young policewoman who wrote poetry in the style of Sylvia Plath, working undercover at *The*

New York Review of Books. But that wasn't going to do me any good. Bloom was a small fish. I was angling for the biggest one of all.

Problem was, I was banging my head against a brick wall and it wasn't for sure which was going to give first. I didn't like to call in debts, but I couldn't put it off any longer. It was time to look up my old friend Jason Epstein. These days he was a big cheese at Random House, but I knew him back when he was a gumshoe at Pinkerton's.

When he showed up at the Royalton on West Forty-fourth Street, I could tell something was wrong.

They had got to him.

"You too, Jason?" It hurt; I couldn't hide that. "Just tell me why. What's in it for you?"

In reply, he dropped a book on my lap that made the Manhattan phone directory look like a pocket diary. "It's called *The Reader's Catalog*," he said, "and it's my baby. It lists every book worth reading."

I was beginning to understand.

He wouldn't meet my eyes. "Look, Slade, I can't afford to make up the *Catalog* from scratch every week. We're talking stability. Critics talk about the literary canon, publishers talk about the importance of a strong backlist, but it comes to the same."

With the help of two waiters, I lifted *The Reader's Catalog* back onto the table. I thought about all the lives that had been ruined to make it possible. I thought about the most respected writers of our time acting like citizens of the Town That Dreaded Sundown. "You've got to give me a name, Jason," I said. There was anger in my voice; fear, too. I didn't care what they'd done to him, didn't care about the things he'd done. I just had to reach him somehow.

Jason didn't say anything for a long while, just watched the ice cubes dissolve in his Aqua Libra.

"I'm taking a big risk just being seen with you," he said, massaging his temples.

But in the end, he came through.

■ ■ ■

So that's what I was doing at ten o'clock in the morning, my trench coat hunched over my head, tailing Susan Sontag down the rainy streets. Epstein told me she was scheduled to make a pickup that morning. If so, she'd lead me where I wanted to go.

My confidence was growing, and I didn't think twice when she strode under the Thirty-eighth Street overpass on the East Side. Vandals had knocked out most of the lights. The darkness protected me, but I had a hard time making her out in the gloom.

Then somebody laid a blackjack to the back of my head and the lights went out completely.

■ ■ ■

When I came to, my head was throbbing and my eyes didn't want to focus. I made them.

Something told me I'd arrived at my destination. I was seated before an enormous desk, ornately carved with claw-and-ball feet. And an enormous tufted leather chair with its back to me.

Slowly, it swiveled around.

The old man was small, and the huge chair made him seem tiny. He winked at me.

"Who are you?" I said. It came out like a croak.

"It's not important," he said blandly. "The organization is what's important."

"Organization?" I was dimly aware of the floor vibrating beneath my feet. Meant we were probably in a factory of some sort.

"The literary canon—now that ain't chopped liver. Could be you don't understand how big this thing is. We've got people all over, wouldn't work otherwise.

We've got the daily reviewers, we've got the head of the teachers' union. . . ."

"Al Shanker? He's with you?"

He seemed amused by my naïveté. "We've got people in the teacher's training colleges. We got the literature profs at your colleges, they're all in on it. The guys who edit the anthologies—Norton, Oxford, you name it—they all work for us. Ever hear about the Trilateral Commission?"

"Something to do with international trade?"

His cheeks dimpled when he smiled. "That's the front. It's really about the literary canon. The usual hustle: we'll read Lady Murasaki if they let in James and Emerson. It's a tricky business, though, when you get into fair-trade issues. We got reports that the English are *dumping*. Some of our guys wanted to use the farm parity system for Anthony Burgess—you know, pay him not to write novels." He rolled his eyes. "Never works. They tried it over here with Joyce Carol Oates. She just sold the overage under a bunch of pseudonyms."

I tried to cluck sympathetically, but it caught in my throat.

"Sooner or later they'll come to me," he said. "And I'll take care of it, like I always do."

"Sounds like a lot of responsibility."

"You see why my boys didn't appreciate your sniffing around. There's too much at stake. You gotta play by the rules." He spread his brown-spotted hands on the desk. "Our rules."

"Who would've thought it? Literary immortality a protection racket."

He mouthed his cigar obscenely. "Come off it, kid. There's no immortality in this business. You want twenty years, even forty, we can arrange it. Beyond that, we'll have to renegotiate terms at the end of the period. Sooner or later there's going to be a, whaddaya call it, reassessment. We send a guy down, he does an appraisal, figures the reputation's not really earned, and bingo, you're out. Maybe you'll get a callback in fifty years or so. Maybe not."

I shook my head. "You guys play hardball." I laughed, but I was scared.

"You see what we did with James Gould Cozzens?"

"Who?"

"Exactly. And thirty years ago, he was the hottest thing around. Then somebody got a little greedy, figured they could cut their own deal. . . ." The old man laughed, showed teeth like little yellow nubbins. "Something I want you to see."

He led me out of his office and onto an inside balcony overlooking a vast industrial atrium. I heard the din of machinery, felt the blast of hot factory air. And I saw the automatic conveyor belt below. At first I thought it was a moving slag heap, but it wasn't. All at once I felt sick and dizzy.

Heaped high on the conveyor belt, thousands and thousands of books were being fed into a belching, grinding mechanical maw.

Turned into pulp.

I could make out only some of the titles. There were fat novels by James Jones and Erskine Caldwell and Thomas Wolfe and James T. Farrell and Pearl Buck. Thin novels by Nelson Algren and William Saroyan. The old Brooks and Warren *Understanding Poetry* nestled beside the collected plays of Clifford Odets. I tried to look away, but my eyes were held by a sick fascination. *Butterfield 8* and *The Big Sky*, *Young Lonigan* and *Manhattan Transfer*, *Darkness at Noon* and *On the Road*—the literary has-beens of our age, together at last, blended into a high-fiber gruel.

The old man led me back into his office and closed the door.

"Beginning to get the picture? You want to take care you don't end up on that pile, Mr. Slade." He squeezed my shoulder and said, "Of course there might be another way."

I shook my head. "You're going to have to kill me," I said.

He opened the left-hand drawer of his desk, removed a dog-eared copy of a journal. "My boys came up with something interesting." It was in *The Dalhousie Review*, Spring 1947. He looked triumphant. "A sestina called 'Cadences of Flight.' Makes you a published poet yourself, doesn't it?"

"Jeepers," I said. My face was hot with embarrassment. "I was in high school."

That's when he made his proposal. I know, Dwight Macdonald said that people who sell out never really had anything to sell, but what did I care? Turned out Dwight was on their payroll from the beginning. Listening to the sound of untold literary tonnage being pulped, I had to admit there were worse things than being co-opted.

■ ■ ■

When I got to my apartment, I dialed Estelle's number and told her she might as well come over. She was at my door in a quarter of an hour, wearing a long gray trench coat with a belt, as heavily made-up as ever.

"Estelle," I said, "I'm off the case." I peeled twenty-five dollars off my billfold. "You can have your money back."

"They turned you, didn't they?" she said, scarlet suffusing her beige pancake foundation.

I looked at her wistfully. The gal had spunk, and I admired that. I felt a sudden rush of warmth toward her. All these years of kicking around the city alone — maybe it was time to settle down with somebody. Sure, her cock-amamie assignment had turned my life upside down, but right then her body looked inviting to my tired eyes. Maybe it was fate that brought us together, I was thinking. Maybe.

I said, "Lookit, everyone's got a price."

"Yeah? What was yours?"

"I'm in, sugar," I blurted. "You understand what I'm saying? They're going to put 'Cadences of Flight' in *The Norton Anthology of Poetry*, fourth edition. It's gonna be deconstructed, reconstructed, and historicized in *PMLA*. And there's going to be a couple of questions about it on the New York State Regents exam in English. It was a take-it-or-leave-it proposition, baby. How could I say no?"

"You were going to blow the whistle on the whole outfit."

"And they were going to feed me into a paper mill. Sometimes you don't know what's in your best interest till someone points it out to you."

The look she gave me was smoldering, and not with passion.

"But Estelle" — and I gazed into her eyes soulfully — "I been thinking maybe we have the rest of our lives together for explanations."

Estelle stared at me for what seemed like a long time. Then she worked her fingers into her hair and started working it free. It was a wig. The eyelashes went next, then she ran a towel under the tap and scrubbed off her makeup. She fished out the stuffed brassiere last of all.

The transformation was astonishing. Before me stood a perfectly ordinary-looking man in his early fifties, his dark hair beginning to gray.

I began to shake. "You're — you're. . . ."

"Thomas Pynchon," he said in a baritone. Pulled off the white gloves and extended a meaty paw.

Thomas Pynchon. Now there was someone you never saw on "Oprah Winfrey."

My mind wanted to reel, but I pulled it in sharp. "So that's why you sent me on this mission impossible."

"I knew you'd never take the case if you knew who I was."

Mists were clearing. "Damn right I wouldn't. Being a famous recluse wasn't good enough for you. It was anonymity you were after. You didn't care if you had to bring down the whole system of dispensation to get it." I paused for breath. "I've got it right, haven't I? That's why you set me up, with this despicable Estelle act."

Pynchon only shrugged.

"So," I said, "you wanted out." The words came out through gritted teeth: "Out of the canon."

"Can you blame a guy for trying?" he asked, and walked out of my life.

Alone in my apartment, I poured myself a couple of fingers of Jack Daniels and tried to make room on my shelves for the critical essays and Ph.D. dissertations about me they said would come flooding in. I was going to be explicated, which was good. I was going to be deconstructed, which wasn't so good. It was a tough job, being a canonical author.

But somebody had to do it.

2

The Master's Pieces: On Canon Formation and the African-American Tradition

William Bennett and Allan Bloom, the dynamic duo of the new cultural right, have become the easy targets of the cultural left — which I am defining here loosely and generously, as that uneasy, shifting set of alliances formed by feminist critics, critics of so-called minority discourse, and Marxist and poststructuralist critics generally, the Rainbow Coalition of contemporary critical theory. These two men symbolize for us the nostalgic return to what I think of as the "antebellum aesthetic position," when men were men, and men were white, when scholar-critics were white men, and when women and persons of color were voiceless, faceless servants and laborers, pouring tea and filling brandy snifters in the boardrooms of old boys' clubs. Inevitably, these two men have come to play the roles for us that George Wallace and Orville Faubus played for the civil rights movement, or that Nixon and Kissinger played for us during Vietnam — the "feel good" targets, who, despite our internal differences and contradictions, we all love to hate.

And how tempting it is to juxtapose their "civilizing mission" to the racial violence that has swept through our campuses since 1986 — at traditionally liberal northern institutions such as the University of Massachusetts at Amherst, Mount Holyoke College, Smith College, the University of Chicago, Columbia, and at southern institutions such as the University of Alabama, the University of Texas, and at the Citadel. Add to this the fact that affirmative action programs on campus have meanwhile become window-dressing operations, necessary "evils" maintained to preserve the fiction of racial fairness and openness, but deprived of the power to enforce their stated principles. When unemployment among black youth is 40 percent, when 44 percent of black Americans can't read the front page of a newspaper, when less than 4 percent of the faculty on campuses is black, well, you look for targets close at hand.

And yet there's a real danger of localizing our grievances, of the easy personification, assigning a celebrated face to the forces of reaction and so giving too much credit to a few men who are really symptomatic of a larger political current. Maybe our eagerness to do so reflects a certain vanity that academic cultural critics are prone to. We make dire predictions, and when they come true, we think we've changed the world.

It's a tendency that puts me in mind of my father's favorite story about Father Divine, that historic con-man of the cloth. In the 1930s he was put on trial for using the mails to defraud, I think, and was convicted. At sentencing, Father Divine stood up and told the judge: I'm warning you, you send me to jail, something terrible is going to happen to you. Father Divine, of course, was sent to prison, and a week later, by sheer coincidence, the judge had a heart attack and died. When the warden and the guards found out about it in the middle of the night, they raced to Father Divine's cell and woke him up. Father Divine, they said, your judge just dropped dead of a heart attack. Without missing a beat, Father Divine lifted his head and told them: "I *hated* to do it."

As writers, teachers, or intellectuals, most of us would like to claim greater efficacy for our labors than we're entitled to. These days, literary criticism likes to think of itself as "war by other means." But it should start to wonder: Have its victories come too easily? The recent move toward politics and history in literary studies has turned the analysis of texts into a marionette theater of the political, to which we bring all the passions of our real-world commitments. And that's why it is sometimes necessary to remind ourselves of the distance from the classroom to the streets. Academic critics write essays, "readings" of literature, where the bad guys (for example, racism or patriarchy) lose, where the forces of oppression are subverted by the boundless powers of irony and allegory that no prison can contain, and we glow with hard-won triumph. We pay homage to the marginalized and demonized, and it feels almost as if we've righted a real-world injustice. I always think of the folktale about the fellow who killed seven with one blow.

Ours was the generation that took over buildings in the late sixties and demanded the creation of black and women's studies programs, and now, like the return of the repressed, has come back to challenge the traditional curriculum. And some of us are even attempting to redefine the canon by editing anthologies. Yet it sometimes seems that blacks are doing better in the college curriculum than they are in the streets.

This is not a defeatist moan. Just an acknowledgment

that the relation between our critical postures and the social struggles they reflect upon is far from transparent. That doesn't mean there's no relation, of course, only that it's a highly mediated one. In any event, I do think we should be clear about when we've swatted a fly and when we've toppled a giant.

In the swaddling clothes of our academic complacencies, few of us are prepared when we bump against something hard, and sooner or later, we do. One of the first talks I ever gave was to a packed audience at the Howard University Honors Seminar, and it was one of those mistakes you don't do twice. Fresh out of graduate school, immersed in the arcane technicalities of contemporary literary theory, I was going to deliver a crunchy structuralist analysis of a slave narrative by Frederick Douglass, tracing the intricate play of its "binary oppositions." Everything was neatly schematized, formalized, analyzed; this was my Sunday-best structuralism, crisp white shirt and shiny black shoes. And it wasn't playing. If you've seen an audience glaze over, this was double-glazing. Bravely, I finished my talk and, of course, asked for questions. Long silence. Finally, a young man in the very back of the room stands up and says, "Yeah, brother, all we want to know is, was Booker T. a Tom or not?"

The funny thing is, this happens to be an interesting question, a lot more interesting than my talk was. And while I didn't exactly appreciate it at the time, the exchange did draw my attention, a little rudely perhaps, to the yawning chasm between our critical discourse and the traditions they discourse on. You know — Is there a canon in this class? People often like to represent the high canonical texts as the reading matter of the power elite. I mean, you have to try to imagine James Baker curling up with the *Four Quartets*, Dan Quayle leafing through the *Princess Cassimassima*. I suppose this is the vision, anyway. What's wrong with this picture? Now, Louis

L'Amour or Ian Fleming, possibly. But that carries us a ways from the high canonical.

When I think back to that Howard talk, I think back to why I went into the study of literature in the first place. I suppose the literary canon is, in no very grand sense, the commonplace book of our shared culture, in which we have written down the texts and titles that we want to remember, that had some special meaning for us. How else did those of us who teach literature fall in love with our subject than through our own commonplace books, in which we inscribed, secretly and privately, as we might do in a diary, those passages of books that named for us what we had for so long deeply felt, but could not say? I kept mine from the age of twelve, turning to it to repeat those marvelous passages that named myself in some private way. From H. H. Munro and O. Henry—I mean, some of the popular literature we had on the shelves at home—to Dickens and Austen, to Hugo and de Maupassant, I found resonant passages that I used to inscribe in my book. Finding James Baldwin and writing him down at an Episcopal church camp during the Watts riots in 1965 (I was fifteen) probably determined the direction of my intellectual life more than did any other single factor. I wrote and rewrote verbatim his elegantly framed paragraphs, full of sentences that were at once somehow Henry Jamesian and King Jamesian, yet clothed in the cadences and figures of the spirituals. I try to remind my graduate students that each of us turned to literature through literal or figurative commonplace books, a fact that we tend to forget once we adopt the alienating strategies of formal analysis. The passages in my commonplace book formed my own canon, just as I imagine each of yours did for you. And a canon, as it has functioned in every literary tradition, has served as the commonplace book of our shared culture.

■   ■   ■

But the question I want to turn to now is this: How does the debate over canon formation affect the development of African-American literature as a subject of instruction in the American academy?

Curiously enough, the first use of the word *canon* in relation to the African-American literary tradition occurs in 1846, in a speech delivered by Theodore Parker. Parker was a theologian, a Unitarian clergyman, and a publicist for ideas, whom Perry Miller described eloquently as "the man who next only to Emerson . . . was to give shape and meaning to the Transcendental movement in America." In a speech on "The Mercantile Classes" delivered in 1846, Parker laments the sad state of "American" letters:

> Literature, science, and art are mainly in [poor men's] hands, yet are controlled by the prevalent spirit of the nation. . . . In England, the national literature favors the church, the crown, the nobility, the prevailing class. Another literature is rising, but is not yet national, *still less canonized.* We have no American literature which is permanent. Our scholarly books are only an imitation of a foreign type; they do not reflect our morals, manners, politics, or religion, not even our rivers, mountains, sky. They have not the smell of our ground in their breath.

Parker, to say the least, was not especially pleased with American letters and their identity with the English tradition. Did Parker find any evidence of a truly American literature?

> The American literature is found only in newspapers and speeches, perhaps in some novel, hot, passionate, but poor and extemporaneous. That is our national literature. Does that favor man — represent man? Certainly not. All is the reflection of this most powerful class. The truths that are told are for them, and the lies. Therein the prevailing sentiment is getting into the form of thoughts.

Parker's analysis, we see plainly, turns upon an implicit reflection theory of base and superstructure. It is the occasional literature, "poor and extemporaneous," wherein "American" literature dwells, but a literature, like English literature, which reflects the interests and ideologies of the upper classes.

Three years later, in his major oration on "The American Scholar," Parker had at last found an entirely original genre of American literature:

> Yet, there is one portion of our permanent literature, if literature it may be called, which is wholly indigenous and original. . . . [W]e have one series of literary productions that could be written by none but Americans, and only here; I mean the Lives of Fugitive Slaves. But as these are not the work of the men of superior culture they hardly help to pay the scholar's debt. Yet all the original romance of Americans is in them, not in the white man's novel.

Parker was right about the originality, the peculiarly *American* quality, of the slave narratives. But he was wrong about their inherent inability to "pay the scholar's debt"; scholars had only to learn to *read* the narratives for their debt to be paid in full. Parker was put off by the language of the slaves' narratives. He would have done well to heed the admonition that Emerson had made in his 1844 speech, "Emancipation in the British West Indies": "Language," Emerson wrote, "must be raked, the secrets of slaughter-houses and infamous holes that cannot front the day, must be ransacked, to tell what negro slavery has been." The narratives, for Parker, were not instances of great literature, but they were a prime site of America's "original romance." As Charles Sumner said in 1852, the fugitive slaves and their narratives "are among the heroes of our age. Romance has no storms of more thrilling interest than theirs. Classical antiquity has preserved no examples of adventurous trial more worthy of renown." Parker's and Sumner's divergent views reveal that the popularity of the narratives in antebellum America most certainly did not reflect any sort of common critical agreement about their nature and status as art. Still, the implications of these observations upon black canon formation would not be lost upon those who would soon seek to free the black slave, or to elevate the ex-slave, through the agency of literary production.

Johann Herder's ideas of the "living spirit of a language" were brought to bear with a vengeance upon eighteenth- and nineteenth-century considerations of the place in nature of the black. Indeed the relationship between the social and political subjectivity of the Negro and the production of art had been discussed by a host of commentators, including Hume, Hegel, and Kant, since Morgan Godwyn wondered aloud about it in 1684. But it was probably Emerson's comments that generated our earliest efforts at canon formation. As Emerson said, again in his speech on "Emancipation in the West Indies":

> If [racial groups] are rude and foolish, down they must go. When at last in a race a new principle appears, an idea — *that* conserves it; ideas only save races. If the black man is feeble and not important to the existing races, not on a parity with the best race, the black man must serve, and be exterminated. But if the black man carries in his bosom an indispensable element of a new and coming civilization; for the sake of that element, no wrong nor strength nor circumstance can hurt him; he will survive and play his part. . . . [N]ow let [the blacks] emerge, clothed and in their own form.

The forms in which they would be clothed would be registered in anthologies that established the canon of black American literature.

The first attempt to define a black canon that I have found is that by Armand Lanusse, who edited *Les Ce-*

nelles, an anthology of black French verse published at New Orleans in 1845 — the first black anthology, I believe, ever published. Lanusse's introduction is a defense of poetry as an enterprise for black people, in their larger efforts to defend the race against "the spiteful and calumnious arrows shot at us," at a target defined as the collective black intellect. Despite this stated political intention, these poems imitate the styles and themes of the French Romantics, and never engage directly the social and political experiences of black Creoles in New Orleans in the 1840s. *Les Cenelles* argues for a political effect — that is, the end of racism — by publishing apolitical poems, poems which share as silent second texts the poetry written by Frenchmen three thousand miles away. We are just like the French — so, treat us like Frenchmen, not like blacks. An apolitical art being put to uses most political.

Four years later, in 1849, William G. Allen published an anthology in which he canonized Phillis Wheatley and George Moses Horton. Like Lanusse, Allen sought to refute intellectual racism by the act of canon formation. "The African's called inferior," he wrote. "But what race has ever displayed intellect more exaltedly, or character more sublime?" Pointing to the achievements of Pushkin, Placido, and Augustine, as the great "African" tradition to which African-Americans were heir, Allen claimed Wheatley and Horton as the exemplars of this tradition, Horton being "decidedly the superior genius," no doubt because of his explicitly racial themes, a judgment quite unlike that which propelled Armand Lanusse into canon formation. As Allen put it, with the publication of their anthology:

Who will now say that the African is incapable of attaining to intellectual or moral greatness? What he now is, degrading circumstances have made him. What he is capable of becoming, the past clearly evinces. The African is strong, tough and hardy. Hundreds of years of oppression have not subdued his spirit, and though Church and State have combined to enslave and degrade him, in spite of them all, he is increasing in strength and power, and in the respect of the entire world.

Here, then, we see the poles of black canon formation, established firmly by 1849: Is "black" poetry racial in theme, or is "black" poetry any sort of poetry written by black people? This quandary has been at play in the tradition ever since.

I won't trace in detail the history of this tension over definitions of the African-American canon, and the direct relation between the production of black poetry and the end of white racism. Suffice it to point to such seminal attempts at canon formation in the 1920s as James Weldon Johnson's *The Book of American Negro Poetry* (1922), Alain Locke's *The New Negro* (1925), and V. F. Calverton's *An Anthology of American Negro Literature* (1929), each of which defined as its goal the demonstration of the existence of the black tradition as a political defense of the racial self against racism. As Johnson put it so clearly:

> A people may be great through many means, but there is only one measure by which its greatness is recognized and acknowledged. The final measure of the greatness of all peoples is the amount and standard of the literature and art that they have produced. The world does not know that a people is great until that people produces great literature and art. No people that has produced great literature and art has ever been looked upon by the world as distinctly inferior.
>
> The status of the Negro in the United States is more a question of national mental attitude toward the race than of actual conditions. And nothing will do more to change that mental attitude and raise his status than a demonstration of intellectual parity by the Negro through the production of literature and art.

Johnson, here, was echoing racialist arguments that had been used against blacks since the eighteenth century, especially those by Hume, Kant, Jefferson, and Hegel, which equated our access to natural rights with our production of literary classics. The Harlem Renaissance, in fact, can be thought of as a sustained attempt to combat racism through the very *production* of black art and literature.

Johnson's and Calverton's anthologies "frame" the Renaissance period, making a comparison between their ideological concerns useful. Calverton's anthology made two significant departures from Johnson's model, both of which are worth considering, if only briefly. Calverton's was the first attempt at black canon formation to provide for the influence and presence of black vernacular literature in a major way. "Spirituals," "Blues," and "Labor Songs" each comprised a genre of black literature for him. We all understand the importance of this gesture and the influence it had upon Sterling Brown, Arthur Davis, and Ulysses Lee, the editors of *The Negro Caravan* (1941). Calverton, whose real name was George Goetz, announced in his introductory essay, "The Growth of Negro Literature," that his selection principles had been determined by his sense of the history of black literary *forms*, leading him to make selections because of their formal "representative value," as he put it. These forms, he continued, were *Negro* forms, virtually self-contained in a hermetic black tradition, especially in the vernacular tradition, where artistic American originality was to be found:

> . . . [I]t is no exaggeration whatsoever to contend that [the Negro's contributions to American art and literature] are more striking and singular in substance and structure than any contributions that have been made by the white man to American culture. In fact, they constitute America's chief claim to originality in its cultural history. . . . The white

man in America has continued, and in an inferior manner, a
culture of European origin. He has not developed a culture
that is definitely and unequivocally American. In respect of
originality, then, the Negro is more important in the growth
of American culture than the white man. . . . While the
white man has gone to Europe for his models, and is seeking
still a European approval of his artistic endeavors, the Negro
in his art forms has never sought the acclaim of any culture
other than his own. This is particularly true of those forms
of Negro art that come directly from the people.

And note that Calverton couched his argument in just
that rhetoric of nationalism, of American exceptionalism,
that had long been used to exclude, or anyway occlude,
the contribution of the Negro. In an audacious reversal,
it turns out that *only* the Negro is really American, the
white man being a pale imitation of his European fore-
bears.

　　If Calverton's stress upon the black vernacular heavily
influenced the shaping of *The Negro Caravan* — certainly
one of the most important anthologies in the tradition —
his sense of the black canon as a formal self-contained
entry most certainly did not. As the editors put it in the
introduction to the volume:

　　　　[We] . . . do not believe that the expression "Negro liter-
　　ature" is an accurate one, and . . . have avoided using it.
　　"Negro literature" has no application if it means structural
　　peculiarity, or a Negro school of writing. The Negro writes
　　in the forms evolved in English and American literature.
　　. . . The editors consider Negro writers to be American writ-
　　ers, and literature by American Negroes to be a segment of
　　American literature. . . .
　　　　The chief cause for objection to the term is that "Negro
　　literature" is too easily placed by certain critics, white and
　　Negro, in an alcove apart. The next step is a double standard
　　of judgment, which is dangerous for the future of Negro

writers. "A Negro novel," thought of as a separate form, is too often condoned as "good enough for a Negro." That Negroes in America have had a hard time, and that inside stories of Negro life often present unusual and attractive reading matter are incontrovertible facts; but when they enter literary criticism these facts do damage to both the critics and artists.

Yet immediately following this stern admonition, we're told the editors haven't been too concerned to maintain "an even level of literary excellence," because the tradition is defined by both form and content:

> Literature by Negro authors about Negro experience . . . must be considered as significant, not only because of a body of established masterpieces, but also because of the illumination it sheds upon a social reality.

And later, in the introduction to the section entitled "The Novel," the editors elaborate upon this idea by complaining about the relation of revision between *Iola Leroy* (1892) and *Clotel* (1853), a relation of the sort central to Calverton's canon, but here defined most disapprovingly: "There are repetitions of situations from Brown's *Clotel,* something of a forecast of a sort of literary inbreeding which causes Negro writers to be influenced by other Negroes more than should ordinarily be expected." The black canon, for these editors, was that literature which most eloquently refuted white racist stereotypes and which embodied the shared "theme of struggle that is present in so much Negro expression." Theirs, in other words, was a canon that was unified thematically by self-defense against racist literary conventions, and by the expression of what the editors called "strokes of freedom." The formal bond that Calverton had claimed was of no academic or political use to these editors, precisely because they wished to project an integrated canon of American literature. As the editors put it:

> [i]n spite of such unifying bonds as a common rejection of the popular stereotypes and a common "racial" cause, writings by Negroes do not seem to the editors to fall into a unique cultural pattern. Negro writers have adopted the literary traditions that seemed useful for their purposes. . . . While Frederick Douglass brought more personal knowledge and bitterness into his antislavery agitation than William Lloyd Garrison and Theodore Parker, he is much closer to them in spirit and in form than to Phillis Wheatley, his predecessor, and Booker T. Washington, his successor. . . . The bonds of literary tradition seem to be stronger than race.

Form, then, or the community of structure and sensibility, was called upon to reveal the sheer arbitrariness of American "racial" classifications, and their irrelevance to American canon formation. Above all else, these editors sought to expose the essentialism at the center of racialized subdivisions of the American literary tradition. If we recall that this anthology appeared just thirteen years before *Brown v. Board*, we should not be surprised by the "integrationist" thrust of the poetics espoused here. Ideological desire and artistic premise were one. African-American literature, then, was a misnomer; "American literature" written by Negroes more aptly designated this body of writing. So much for a definition of the African-American tradition based on formal relationships of revision, text to text.

At the opposite extreme in black canon formation is the canon defined by Amiri Baraka and Larry Neal in *Black Fire*, published in 1968, an anthology so very familiar to us all. This canon, the blackest canon of all, was defined both by formal innovations and by themes: formally, individual selections tend to aspire to the vernacular or to black music, or to performance; theoretically, each selection reinforces the urge toward black liberation, toward "freedom now" with an up-against-the-wall subtext. The hero, the valorized presence in this volume, is the black vernacular: no longer summoned or invoked through familiar and comfortable rubrics such as "The Spirituals" and "The Blues," but *embodied, assumed, presupposed* in a marvelous act of formal bonding often obscured by the stridency of the political message the anthology meant to announce. Absent completely was a desire to "prove" our common humanity with white people, by demonstrating our power of intellect. One mode of essentialism — "African" essentialism — was used to critique the essentialism implicit in notions of a common or universal American heritage. No, in *Black Fire*, art and act were one.

■ ■ ■

I have been thinking about these strains in black canon formation because a group of us will be editing still another anthology, which will constitute still another attempt at canon formation: W. W. Norton will be publishing the *Norton Anthology of African-American Literature*. The editing of this anthology has been a great dream of mine for a long time. After a year of readers' reports, market surveys, and draft proposals, Norton has enthusiastically embarked upon the publishing of our anthology.

I think that I am most excited about the fact that we will have at our disposal the means to edit an anthology that will define a canon of African-American literature for instructors and students at any institution which desires to teach a course in African-American literature. Once our anthology is published, no one will ever again be able to use the unavailability of black texts as an excuse not to teach our literature. A well-marked anthology functions in the academy to *create* a tradition, as well as to define and preserve it. A Norton anthology opens up a

literary tradition as simply as opening the cover of a carefully edited and ample book.

I am not unaware of the politics and ironies of canon
formation. The canon that we define will be "our" canon,
one possible set of selections among several possible sets of
selections. In part to be as eclectic and as democratically
"representative" as possible, most other editors of black
anthologies have tried to include as many authors and
selections (especially excerpts) as possible, in order to preserve and "resurrect" the tradition. I call this the Sears
and Roebuck approach, the "dream book" of black literature.

We have all benefited from this approach to collection. Indeed, many of our authors have managed to survive only because an enterprising editor was determined
to marshal as much evidence as she or he could to show
that the black literary tradition existed. While we must
be deeply appreciative of that approach and its results,
our task will be a different one.

Our task will be to bring together the "essential" texts
of the canon, the "crucially central" authors, those whom
we feel to be indispensable to an understanding of the
shape, and shaping, of the tradition. A canon is often
represented as the "essence" of the tradition, indeed, as
the marrow of tradition: the connection between the texts
of the canon is meant to reveal the tradition's inherent,
or veiled, logic, its internal rationale.

None of us is naive enough to believe that "the canonical" is self-evident, absolute, or neutral. It is a commonplace of contemporary criticism to say that scholars make
canons. But, just as often, writers make canons, too, both
by critical revaluation and by reclamation through revision. Keenly aware of this — and, quite frankly, aware of
my own biases — I have attempted to bring together a
group of scholar-critics whose notions of the black canon
might not necessarily agree with my own, or with each

others'. I have tried to bring together a diverse array of ideological, methodological, and theoretical perspectives, so that we together might produce an anthology that most fully represents the various definitions of what it means to speak of an African-American literary tradition, and what it means to *teach* that tradition. And while we are at the earliest stages of organization, I can say that my own biases toward canon formation are to stress the formal relationships that obtain among texts in the black tradition — relations of revision, echo, call and response, antiphony, what have you — and to stress the vernacular roots of the tradition. For the vernacular, or oral literature, in our tradition, has a canon of its own.

But my pursuit of this project has required me to negotiate a position between, on the one hand, William Bennett, who claims that black people can have no canon, no masterpieces, and, on the other hand, those on the critical left who wonder why we want to establish the existence of a canon, any canon, in the first place. On the right hand, we face the outraged reactions of those custodians of Western culture who protest that the canon, that transparent decanter of Western values, may become — breathe the word — *politicized*. But the only way to answer the charge of "politics" is with an emphatic *tu quoque*. That people can maintain a straight face while they protest the irruption of politics into something that has always been political from the beginning — well, it says something about how remarkably successful official literary histories have been in presenting themselves as natural and neutral objects, untainted by worldly interests.

I agree with those conservatives who have raised the alarm about our students' ignorance of history. But part of the history we need to teach has to be the history of the idea of the "canon," which involves (though it's hardly exhausted by) the history of literary pedagogy and of the institution of the school. Once we understand how they arose, we no longer see literary canons as *objets trouvés* washed up on the beach of history. And we can begin to appreciate their ever-changing configuration in relation to a distinctive institutional history.

Universal education in this country was justified by the argument that schooling made good citizens, good American citizens; and when American literature started to be taught in our schools, part of the aim was to show what it was to be an American. As Richard Brodhead, a leading scholar of American literature, has observed, "no past lives without cultural mediation. The past, however worthy, does not survive by its own intrinsic power." One function of "literary history" is, then, to disguise that mediation, to conceal all connections between institution-alized interests and the literature we remember. Pay no attention to the man behind the curtain, booms the Great Oz of literary history.

Cynthia Ozick once chastised feminists by warning that *strategies become institutions*. But isn't that really another way of warning that their strategies, heaven for-fend, may *succeed?* Here we approach the scruples of those on the cultural left, who worry about, well, the price of success. "Who's co-opting whom?" might be their slogan. To them, the very idea of the canon is hierarchi-cal, patriarchal, and otherwise politically suspect. They'd like us to disavow it altogether.

But history and its institutions are not just something we study, they're also something we live, and live through. And how effective and how durable our inter-ventions in contemporary cultural politics will be de-pends upon our ability to mobilize the institutions that buttress and reproduce that culture. The choice isn't be-tween institutions and no institutions. The choice is al-ways: What kind of institutions shall there be? Fearing that our strategies will become institutions, we could seclude ourselves from the real world and keep our hands clean, free from the taint of history. But that is to pay obeisance to the status quo, to the entrenched arsenal of sexual and racial authority, to say that they shouldn't change, become something other, and, let's hope, better than they are now.

Indeed, this is one case where we've got to borrow a leaf from the right, which is exemplarily aware of the role of education in the reproduction of values. We must engage in this sort of canon deformation precisely because Mr. Bennett is correct: the teaching of literature *is* the teaching of values; not inherently, no, but contingently, yes; it is—it has become—the teaching of an aesthetic and political order, in which no women or people of color were ever able to discover the reflection or representation of their images, or hear the resonances of their cultural voices. The return of "the" canon, the high canon of Western masterpieces, represents the return of an order in which my people were the subjugated, the voiceless, the invisible, the unrepresented, and the unrepresentable. Who would return us to that medieval never-never land?

The classic critique of our attempts to reconstitute our own subjectivity, as women, as blacks, etc., is that of Jacques Derrida: "This is the risk. The effect of Law is to build a structure of the subject, and as soon as you say, 'well, the woman is a subject and this subject deserves equal rights,' and so on—then you are caught in the logic of phallocentricism and you have rebuilt the empire of Law." To expressions such as this, made by a critic whose stands on sexism and racism have been exemplary, we must respond that the Western male subject has long been constituted historically for himself and in himself. And, while we readily accept, acknowledge, and partake of the critique of *this* subject as transcendent, to deny us the process of exploring and reclaiming our subjectivity

before we critique it is the critical version of the grandfather clause, the double privileging of categories that
happen to be *preconstituted*. Such a position leaves us
nowhere, invisible and voiceless in the republic of Western letters. Consider the irony: precisely when we (and
other Third World peoples) obtain the complex where-
withal to define our black subjectivity in the republic of
Western letters, our theoretical colleagues declare that
there ain't no such thing as a subject, so why should we
be bothered with that? In this way, those of us in feminist
criticism or African-American criticism who are engaged
in the necessary work of canon deformation and reforma-
tion confront the skepticism even of those who are allies
on other fronts, over this matter of the death of the subject and our own discursive subjectivity.

So far I've been talking about social identity and political agency as if they were logically connected. I think
they are. And that has a lot to do with what I think the
task of the critic today must be.

Simone de Beauvoir wrote that one is not born a
woman; no, and one is not born a Negro; but then, as
Donna Haraway has pointed out, one isn't even born an
organism. Lord knows that black art has been attacked
for well over a century as being "not universal," though
no one ever says quite what this might mean. If this
means an attack against *self-identification*, then I must
confess that I am opposed to "universality." This line of
argument is an echo from the political right. As Allan
Bloom wrote:

> . . . [T]he substantial human contact, indifferent to race,
> soul to soul, that prevails in all other aspects of student life
> simply does not usually exist between the two races. There
> are exceptions, perfectly integrated black students, but they
> are rare and in a difficult position. I do not believe this
> somber situation is the fault of the white students who are

rather straightforward in such matters and frequently em-
barrassingly eager to prove their liberal credentials in the
one area where Americans are especially sensitive to a history
of past injustice. . . . Thus, just at the moment when everyone else has become "a person," blacks have become blacks.
. . . "They stick together" was a phrase once used by the
prejudiced, by this or that distinctive group, but it has become true by and large of the black students.

Self-identification proves a condition for agency, for social change. And to benefit from such collective agency,
we need to construct ourselves, just as the nation was
constructed, just as the class was, just as *all* the furniture
in the social universe was. It's utopian to think we can
now disavow our social identities; there's not another one
to take its place. You can't opt out of a Form of Life. We
can't become one of those bodiless vapor trails of sentience
portrayed on that "Star Trek" episode, though often it
seems as if the universalists want us to be just that. You
can't opt out of history. History may be a nightmare, as
Joyce suggested, but it's time to stop pinching ourselves.

But there's a treacherous non sequitur here, from "socially constructed" to essentially unreal. I suppose there's
a lurking positivism in the sentiment, in which social facts
are unreal compared to putatively biological ones. We
go from "constructed" to "unstable," which is one non
sequitur; or to "changeable by will," which is a bigger
problem still, since the "will" is yet another construction.

And theory is conducive to these slippages, however
illegitimate, because of the real ascendancy of the paradigm of dismantlement. Reversals don't work, we're told;
dismantle the scheme of difference altogether. And I
don't deny the importance, on the level of theory, of the
project; it's important to remember that "race" is *only* a
sociopolitical category, nothing more. At the same time —
in terms of its practical performative force — that doesn't

help me when I'm trying to get a taxi on the corner of 125th and Lenox Avenue. ("Please sir, it's only a metaphor.")

Maybe the most important thing here is the tension between the imperatives of agency and the rhetoric of dismantlement. An example: Foucault says, and let's take him at his word, that the "homosexual" as life form was invented sometime in the mid-nineteenth century. Now, if there's no such thing as a homosexual, then homophobia, at least as directed toward people rather than acts, loses its rationale. But you can't respond to the discrimination against gay people by saying, "I'm sorry, I don't exist; you've got the wrong guy." The simple historical fact is, Stonewall was necessary, concerted action was necessary to take action against the very structures that, as it were, called the homosexual into being, that subjected certain people to this imaginary identity. To reverse Audre Lorde, *only* the master's tools will ever dismantle the master's house.

Let me be specific. Those of us working in my own tradition confront the hegemony of the Western tradition, generally, and of the larger American tradition, specifically, as we set about theorizing about our tradition, and engaging in attempts at canon formation. Long after white American literature has been anthologized and canonized, and recanonized, our attempts to define a black American canon, foregrounded on its own against a white backdrop, are often decried as racist, separatist, nationalist, or "essentialist." Attempts to derive theories about our literary tradition from the black tradition — a tradition, I might add, that must include black vernacular forms as well as written literary forms — are often greeted by our colleagues in traditional literature departments as misguided attempts to secede from a union which only recently, and with considerable kicking and screaming, has been forged. What is *wrong* with you people, our friends ask us in genuine passion and concern; after all, aren't we all just citizens of literature here?

Well, yes and no. It is clear that every black American text must confess to a complex ancestry, one high and low (literary and vernacular), but also one white and black. There can be no doubt that white texts inform and influence black texts (and vice versa), so that a thoroughly integrated canon of American literature is not only politically sound, it is *intellectually* sound as well. But the attempts of scholars such as Arnold Rampersad, Houston Baker, M. H. Washington, Nellie McKay, and others to define a black American canon, and to pursue literary interpretation from within this canon, are not meant to refute the soundness of these gestures of integration. Rather, it is a question of perspective, a question of emphasis. Just as we can and must cite a black text within the larger American tradition, we can and must cite it within its own tradition, a tradition not defined by a pseudoscience of racial biology, or a mystically shared essence called blackness, but by the repetition and revision of shared themes, topoi, and tropes, a process that binds the signal texts of the black tradition into a canon just as surely as separate links bind together into a chain. It is no more, or less, essentialist to make this claim than it is to claim the existence of French, English, German, Russian, or American literature — as long as we proceed inductively, from the texts to the theory. For nationalism has always been the dwarf in the critical, canonical chess machine. For anyone to deny us the right to engage in attempts to constitute ourselves as discursive subjects is for them to engage in the double privileging of categories that happen to be preconstituted.

In our attempts at canon formation we are demanding a return to history in a manner scarcely conceived of by the new historicists. Nor can we opt out of our own private histories, which Houston Baker calls the African-American autobiographical moment, and which I call the autocritography. Let me end, as I began, with an anecdote, one that I had forgotten for so long until just the other day.

Recently at Cornell, I was listening to Hortense Spillers, the great black feminist critic, read her important essay, "Mama's Baby, Papa's Maybe." Her delivery, as usual, was flawless, compelling, inimitable. And although I had read this essay as a manuscript, I had never before felt — or heard — the following lines:

> The African-American male has been touched, therefore, by the *mother*, handled by her in ways that he cannot escape, and in ways that the white American male is allowed to temporize by a fatherly reprieve. This human and historic development — the text that has been inscribed on the benighted heart of the continent — takes us to the center of an inexorable difference in the depths of American women's community: the African-American woman, the mother, the daughter, becomes historically the powerful and shadowy evocation of a cultural synthesis long evaporated — the law of the Mother — only and precisely because legal enslavement removed the African-American male not so much from sight as from *mimetic* view as a partner in the prevailing social fiction of the Father's name, the Father's law.
>
> Therefore, the female, in this order of things, breaks in upon the imagination with a forcefulness that marks both a denial and an "illegitimacy." Because of this peculiar American denial, the black American male embodies the *only* American community of males which has had the specific occasion to learn *who* the female is within itself, the infant child who bears the life against the could-be fateful gamble, against the odds of pulverization and murder, including her own. It is the heritage of the *mother* that the African-American male must regain as an aspect of his own personhood — the power of "yes" to the "female" within.

How curious a figure — men, black men, gaining their voices through the black mother. Precisely when some

committed feminists or some committed black nationalists would essentialize all "others" out of their critical
endeavor, Hortense Spillers rejects that glib and easy so-
lution, calling for a revoicing of the "master's" discourse
in the cadences and timbres of the Black Mother's voice.

As I sat there before her, I recalled, to my own astonishment, my own first public performance, when I
was a child of four years. My mom attended a small black
Methodist Church in Piedmont, West Virginia, just as
her mom had done for the past fifty years. I was a fat
little kid, a condition that my mom defended as "plump."
I remember that I had just been given a brand new gray
suit for the occasion, and a black stringy-brim Dobbs hat,
so it must have been Easter, because my brother and I
always got new hats for Easter, just as my dad and mom
did.

At any rate, the day came to deliver my Piece. What
is a Piece? A Piece is what people in our church called a
religious recitation. I don't know what the folk etymology
might be, but I think it reflects the belief that each of the
fragments of our praise songs, taken together, amounts
to a Master Text. And each of us, during a religious program, was called upon to say our Piece. Mine, if you can
believe it, was "Jesus was a boy like me, and like Him I
want to be." That was it—I was only four. So, after
weeks of practice in elocution, hair pressed and greased
down, shirt starched and pants pressed, I was ready to
give my Piece.

I remember skipping along to the church with all
the other kids, driving everyone crazy, saying over and
over, "Jesus was a boy like me, and like Him I want to
be." "Will you shut up!" my friends demanded. Just jeal-
ous, I thought. They probably don't even know their
Pieces.

Finally, we made it to the church, and it was
packed—bulging and glistening with black people, eager
to hear Pieces, despite the fact that they heard all of the

Pieces already, year after year, bits and fragments of a repeated Master Text.

Because I was the youngest child on the program, I was the first to go. Miss Sarah Russell (whom we called Sister Holy Ghost — behind her back, of course) started the program with a prayer, then asked if little Skippy Gates would step forward. I did so.

And then the worst happened: I completely forgot the words of my Piece. Standing there, pressed and starched, just as clean as I could be, in front of just about everybody in our part of town, I could not for the life of me remember one word of that Piece.

After standing there I don't know how long, struck dumb and captivated by all of those staring eyes, I heard a voice from near the back of the church proclaim, "Jesus was a boy like me, and like Him I want to be."

And my mother, having arisen to find my voice, smoothed her dress and sat down again. The congregation's applause lasted as long as its laughter as I crawled back to my seat.

For me, I realized as Hortense Spillers spoke, much of my scholarly and critical work has been an attempt to learn how to speak in the strong, compelling cadences of my mother's voice. To reform core curricula, to account for the comparable eloquence of the African, the Asian, and the Middle Eastern traditions, is to begin to prepare our students for their roles as citizens of a world culture, educated through a truly human notion of "the humanities," rather than — as Bennett and Bloom would have it — as guardians at the last frontier outpost of white male Western culture, the Keepers of the Master's Pieces. And for us as scholar-critics, learning to speak in the voice of the black female is perhaps the ultimate challenge of producing a discourse of the critical Other.

3

Writing, "Race," and the Difference It Makes

The truth is that, with the fading of the Renaissance ideal through progressive stages of specialism, leading to intellectual emptiness, we are left with a potentially suicidal movement among "leaders of the profession," while, at the same time, the profession sprawls, without its old center, in helpless disarray.

One quickly cited example is the professional organization, the Modern Language Association. . . . A glance at its thick program for its last meeting shows a massive increase and fragmentation into more than 500 categories! I cite a few examples: . . . "The Trickster Figure in Chicano and Black Literature." . . . Naturally, the progressive trivialization of topics has made these meetings a laughingstock in the national press.

— W. JACKSON BATE

. . . language, for the individual consciousness, lies on the borderline between oneself and the other. The word in language is half someone else's. It becomes "one's own" only when the speaker populates it with his own intention, his own accent, when he appropriates the word, adapting it to his own semantic and expressive intention. Prior to this moment of appropriation, the word does not exist in a

neutral and impersonal language (it is not, after all,
out of a dictionary that the speaker gets his words!),
but rather it exists in other people's mouths, in other
people's contexts, serving other people's intentions:
it is from there that one must take the word, and
make it "one's own."
— MIKHAIL BAKHTIN

They cannot represent themselves; they must be
represented.
— MARX

I

O f what import is "race" as a meaningful category in
the study of literature and the shaping of critical theory? If we attempt to answer this question by examining
the history of Western literature and its criticism, our
initial response would ostensibly be "nothing," or at the
very least, "nothing explicitly." Indeed, until the past
decade or so, even the most subtle and sensitive literary
critics would most probably have argued that, except for
aberrant moments in the history of criticism, "race" has
been brought to bear upon the study of literature in no
apparent way. The Western literary tradition, after all,
and the canonical texts that comprise this splendid tradition, has been defined since Eliot as a more-or-less closed
set of works that somehow speak to, or respond to, the
"human condition" and to each other in formal patterns
of repetition and revision. And while judgment is subject
to the moment and indeed does reflect temporal-specific
presuppositions, certain works seem to transcend value
judgments of the moment, speaking irresistibly to the
"human condition." The question of the place of texts

written by "the Other" (be that odd metaphor defined as African, Arabic, Chinese, Latin American, female, or Yiddish authors) in the proper study of "literature," "Western literature," or "comparative literature" has, until recently, remained an unasked question, suspended or silenced by a discourse in which the "canonical" and the "noncanonical" stand as the ultimate opposition. "Race," in much of the thinking about the proper study of literature in this century, has been an invisible quality, present implicitly at best.

This was not always the case, of course. By the middle of the nineteenth century, "national spirit" and "historical period" had become widely accepted metaphors within theories of the nature and function of literature which argued that the principal value in a "great" work of literary art resided in the extent to which these categories were *reflected* in that work of art. Montesquieu's *Esprit des lois* had made a culture's formal social institution the repository of its "guiding spirit," while Vico's *Principii d'una scienza nuova* had read literature against a complex pattern of historical cycles. The two Schlegels managed rather deftly to bring to bear upon the interpretation of literature "both national spirit and historical period," as Walter Jackson Bate has shown. But it was Taine who made the implicit explicit by postulating "race, moment, and *milieu*" as positivistic criteria through which any work could be read, and which, by definition, any work reflected. Taine's *History of English Literature* is the great foundation upon which subsequent nineteenth-century notions of "national literatures" would be constructed.

What Taine called "race" was the source of all structures of feeling. To "track the root of man," he wrote, "is to consider the race itself, . . . the structure of his character and mind, his general processes of thought and feeling, . . . the irregularity and revolutions of his conception, which arrest in him the birth of fair dispositions and harmonious forms, the disdain of appearances, the desire for truth, the attachment for bare and abstract ideas, which develop in him conscience, at the expense of all else." In "race," Taine concluded, was predetermined "a particularity inseparable from all the motions of his intellect and his heart. Here lie the grand causes, for they are the universal and permanent causes, . . . indestructible, and finally infallibly supreme." "Poetries," as Taine put it, and all other forms of social expression, "are in fact only the imprints stamped by their seal."

"Race," for Taine was "the first and richest source of these master faculties from which historical events take their rise"; it was a "community of blood and intellect which to this day binds its off-shoots together." Lest we misunderstand the *naturally* determining role of "race," Taine concluded that it "is no simple spring but a kind of lake, a deep reservoir wherein other springs have, for a multitude of centuries, discharged their several streams."

Taine's originality lay not in these ideas about the nature and role of race, but in their almost "scientific" application to the history of literature. These ideas about race were received from the Enlightenment, if not from the Renaissance. By midpoint in the nineteenth century, ideas of irresistible racial differences were commonly held: when Abraham Lincoln invited a small group of black leaders to the White House in 1862 to share with them his ideas about returning all blacks in America to Africa, his argument turned upon these "natural" differences. "You and we are different races," he said. "We have between us a broader difference than exists between any other two races." Since this sense of difference was never to be bridged, Lincoln concluded, the slaves and the ex-slaves should be returned to their own. The growth of canonical "national" literatures was coterminous with the shared assumption among intellectuals that "race"

was a "thing," an ineffaceable quantity, which irresistibly determined the shape and contour of thought and
feelings as surely as it did the shape and contour of human
anatomy.

How did the great movement away from "race, moment, and *milieu*" and toward the language of the text in
the 1920s and 1930s in the Practical Criticism movement
at Cambridge and the New Criticism movement at Yale
affect this category of "race" in the reading of literature?
Race, along with all sorts of other unseemly or untoward
notions about the composition of the literary work of art,
was bracketed or suspended. Race, within these theories
of literature to which we are all heir, was rendered *implicit* in the elevation of ideas of canonical *cultural* texts
that comprise the Western tradition in Eliot's simultaneous order, with a simultaneous existence. History, *milieu,*
and even moment were brought to bear upon the interpretation of literature through philology and etymology:
the dictionary—in the Anglo-American tradition, the *Oxford English Dictionary*—was the castle in which Taine's
criteria took refuge. Once the concept of value became
encased in the belief in a canon of texts whose authors
purportedly shared a "common culture" inherited from
both the Greco-Roman and the Judeo-Christian traditions, no one need speak of matters of "race" since "the
race" of these authors was "the same." One not heir to
these traditions was, by definition, of another "race."
This logic was impenetrable.

Despite their beliefs in the unassailable primacy of
language in the estimation of a work of literature, however, both I. A. Richards and Allen Tate, in separate
prefaces to books of poems by black authors, paused to
wonder aloud about the black faces of the authors, and
the import this had upon the reading of their texts. The
often claimed "racism" of the Southern Agrarians, while
an easily identifiable target, was only an explicit manifes-

tation of presuppositions that formed a large segment of
the foundation upon which formalism was built. The citizens of the republic of literature, in other words, were
all white, and mostly male. Difference, if difference
obtained at all, was a difference obliterated by the "si-
multaneity"of Eliot's "tradition." Eliot's fiction of tradition, for the writer of a culture of color, was the literary
equivalent of the "grandfather clause." So, in response
to Robert Penn Warren's statement in "Pondy Woods"—
"Nigger, your breed ain't metaphysical"—Sterling A.
Brown wrote, "Cracker, your breed ain't exegetical." The
Signifyin(g) pun deconstructed the "racialism" inherent
in these claims of tradition.

II

"Race" as a meaningful criterion within the biological
sciences has long been recognized to be a fiction. When
we speak of the "white race" or the "black race," the
"Jewish race" or the "Aryan race," we speak in misno-
mers, biologically, and in metaphors, more generally.
Nevertheless, our conversations are replete with usages of
race which have their sources in the dubious pseudoscience of the eighteenth and nineteenth centuries. One
need only flip through the pages of the *New York Times*
to find headlines such as "Brown University President
Sees School Racial Problems," or "Sensing Racism, Thousands March in Paris." In a lead editorial of its March
29, 1985, number, "The Lost White Tribe," the *Times*
notes that while "racism is not unique to South Africa,"
we must condemn that society because "Betraying the
religious tenets underlying Western culture, it has made
race the touchstone of political rights." Eliot's "dissociation of sensibility," caused in large part by the "fraternal"
atrocities of the World War I, and then by the inexpli-
cable and insane murder of European Jews two decades

later, the *Times* editorial echoes. (For millions of people who originated outside Europe, however, this dissociation of sensibility had its origins in colonialism and human slavery.) *Race,* in these usages, pretends to be an objective term of classification, when in fact it is a trope.

The sense of difference defined in popular usages of the term *race* has been used both to describe and *inscribe* differences of language, belief system, artistic tradition, "gene pool," and all sorts of supposedly "natural" attributes such as rhythm, athletic ability, cerebration, usury, and fidelity. The relation between "racial character" and these sorts of "characteristics" has been inscribed through tropes of race, lending to even supposedly "innocent" descriptions of cultural tendencies and differences the sanction of God, biology, or the natural order. "Race consciousness," Zora Neale Hurston wrote, "is a deadly explosive on the tongues of men." I even heard a member of the House of Lords in 1973 describe the differences between Irish Protestants and Catholics in terms of their "distinct and clearly definable differences of race."

"You mean to say that you can tell them apart?" I asked incredulously.

"Of course," responded the lord. "Any Englishman can."

Race has become a trope of ultimate, irreducible difference between cultures, linguistic groups, or practitioners of specific belief systems, who more often than not have fundamentally opposed economic interests. Race is the ultimate trope of difference because it is so very arbitrary in its application. The sanction of biology contained in sexual difference, simply put, does not and can never obtain when one is speaking of "racial difference." Yet, we carelessly use language in such a way as to *will* this sense of *natural* difference into our formulations. To do so is to engage in a pernicious act of language, one which exacerbates the complex problem of cultural or "ethnic" difference, rather than assuages or redresses it. This is especially the case at a time when racism has become fashionable, once again. That, literally every day, scores of people are killed in the name of differences ascribed to "race" only makes even more imperative this gesture to "deconstruct," if you will, the ideas of difference inscribed in the trope of race, to take discourse itself as our common subject to be explicated to reveal the latent relations of power and knowledge inherent in popular and academic usages of "race." When twenty-five thousand people feel compelled to gather on the Rue de Rivoli in support of the antiracist "Ne touche pas à mon pote" movement, when thousands of people willingly accept arrest to protest apartheid, when Iran and Iraq feel justified in murdering the other's citizens because of their "race," when Beirut stands as a museum of shards and pieces reflecting degrees of horror impossible to comprehend, the gesture that we make here seems local and tiny.

There is a curious dialectic between formal language use and the inscription of metaphorical "racial" differences. At times, as Nancy Stepan expertly shows in *The Idea of Race in Science*, these metaphors have sought a universal and transcendent sanction in biological science. Western writers in French, Spanish, German, Portuguese, and English have sought to make literal these rhetorical figures of "race," to make them natural, absolute, essential. In doing so, they have *inscribed* these differences as fixed and finite categories which they merely report or draw upon for authority. But it takes little reflection to recognize that these pseudoscientific categories are themselves figures of thought. Who has seen a black or red person, a white, yellow, or brown? These terms are arbitrary constructs, not reports of reality. But language is not only the medium of this often pernicious tendency, it is its *sign*. Language use signifies the difference between cultures and their possession of power, spelling the difference between subordinate and superordinate, between bondsman and lord. Its call into use is simultaneous with the shaping of an economic order in which the cultures of color have been dominated in several important senses by Western Judeo-Christian, Greco-Hellenic cultures and their traditions. To use contemporary theories of criticism to explicate these modes of inscription is to demystify large and obscure ideological relations and indeed theory itself. It would be useful here to consider a signal example of the black tradition's confinement and delimitation by the commodity of writing. For literacy, as I hope to demonstrate, could be the most pervasive emblem of capitalist commodity functions.

III

Where better to test this thesis than in the example of the black tradition's first poet in English, the African slave girl Phillis Wheatley. Let us imagine a scene:

One bright morning in the spring of 1772, a young African girl walked demurely into the courthouse at Boston, to undergo an oral examination, the results of which would determine the direction of her life and work. Perhaps she was shocked upon entering the appointed room. For there, gathered in a semicircle, sat eighteen of Boston's most notable citizens. Among them was John Erving, a prominent Boston merchant; the Reverend Charles Chauncey, pastor of the Tenth Congregational Church and a son of Cotton Mather; and John Hancock, who would later gain fame for his signature on the Declaration of Independence. At the center of this group would have sat His Excellency, Thomas Hutchinson, governor of the colony, with Andrew Oliver, his lieutenant governor, close by his side.

Why had this august group been assembled? Why had

it seen fit to summon this young African girl, scarcely eighteen years old, before it? This group of "the most respectable characters in *Boston*," as it would later define itself, had assembled to question the African adolescent closely on the slender sheaf of poems that the young woman claimed to have written by herself. We can only speculate on the nature of the questions posed to the fledgling poet. Perhaps they asked her to explain for all to hear exactly who were the Greek and Latin gods and poets alluded to so frequently in her work. Or perhaps they asked her to conjugate a verb in Latin, or even to translate randomly selected passages from the Latin, which she and her master, John Wheatley, claimed that she "had made some progress in." Or perhaps they asked her to recite from memory key passages from the texts of Milton and Pope, the two poets by whom the African claimed to be most directly influenced. We do not know.

We do know, however, that the African poet's responses were more than sufficient to prompt the eighteen august gentlemen to compose, sign, and publish a two-paragraph "Attestation," an open letter "To the Publick" that prefaces Phillis Wheatley's book, and which reads in part:

> We whose Names are underwritten, do assure the World, that the poems specified in the following Page, were (as we veribly believe) written by Phillis, a young Negro Girl, who was but a few Years since, brought an unculti-vated Barbarian from *Africa*, and has ever since been, and now is, under the Disadvantage of serving as a Slave in a Family in this Town. She has been examined by some of the best judges, and is thought qualified to write them.

So important was this document in securing a publisher for Phillis's poems that it forms the signal element in the prefatory matter printed in the opening pages of her

Poems on Various Subjects, Religious and Moral, published at London in 1773.

Without the published "Attestation," Wheatley's publisher claimed, few would believe that an African could possibly have written poetry all by herself. As the eighteen put the matter clearly in their letter, "Numbers would be ready to suspect they were not really the Writings of Phillis." Phillis's master, John Wheatley, and Phillis had attempted to publish a similar volume in 1770 at Boston, but Boston publishers had been incredulous. Three years later, "Attestation" in hand, Phillis and her mistress's son, Nathaniel Wheatley, sailed for England, where they completed arrangements for the publication of a volume of her poems, with the aid of the Countess of Huntington and the Earl of Dartmouth.

This curious anecdote, surely one of the oddest oral examinations on record, is only a tiny part of a larger, and even more curious, episode in the eighteenth century's Enlightenment. At least since 1600, Europeans had wondered aloud whether or not the African "species of men," as they most commonly put it, *could* ever create formal literature, could ever master the "arts and sciences." If they could, the argument ran, then the African variety of humanity and the European variety were fundamentally related. If not, then it seemed clear that the African was destined by nature to be a slave.

Determined to discover the answer to this crucial quandary, several Europeans and Americans undertook experiments in which young African slaves were tutored and trained along with white children. Phillis Wheatley was merely one result of such an experiment. Francis Williams, a Jamaican who took the B.A. at the University of Cambridge before 1730; Jacobus Capitein, who earned several degrees in Holland; Wilheim Amo, who took the doctorate degree in philosophy at Halle; and Ignatius

Sancho, who became a friend of Sterne's and who published a volume of letters in 1782 — these were just a few of the black subjects of such "experiments." The published writings of these black men and one woman, who wrote in Latin, Dutch, German, and English, were seized upon both by pro- and antislavery proponents as proof that their arguments were sound.

So widespread was the debate over "the nature of the African" between 1730 and 1830 that not until the Harlem Renaissance would the work of black writers be as extensively reviewed as it was in the eighteenth century. Phillis Wheatley's list of reviewers includes Votaire, Thomas Jefferson, George Washington, Samuel Rush, and James Beatty, to name only a few. Francis William's work was analyzed by no less than David Hume and Immanuel Kant. Hegel, writing in the *Philosophy of History* in 1813, used the writings of these Africans as the sign of their innate inferiority. The list of commentators is extensive, amounting to a "Who's Who" of the French, English, and American Enlightenment.

Why was the *creative writing* of the African of such importance to the eighteenth century's debate over slavery? I can briefly outline one thesis: After Descartes, *reason* was privileged, or valorized, among all other human characteristics. Writing, especially after the printing press became so widespread, was taken to be the *visible* sign of reason. Blacks were "reasonable," and hence "men," if — and only if — they demonstrated mastery of the "arts and sciences," the eighteenth century's formula for writing. So, while the Enlightenment is famous for establishing its existence upon the human ability to reason, it simultaneously used the absence and presence of "reason" to delimit and circumscribe the very humanity of the cultures and people of color which Europeans had been "discovering" since the Renaissance. The urge toward the systematization of all human knowledge, by which we characterize the Enlightenment, led directly to the relegation of black people to a lower rung on the Great Chain of Being, an eighteenth-century construct that arranged all of creation on a vertical scale from animals and plants and insects through humans to the angels and God himself.

By 1750, the chain had become individualized; the human scale slid from "the lowliest Hottentot" (black south Africans) to "glorious Milton and Newton." If blacks could write and publish imaginative literature, then they could, in effect, take a few Giant Steps up the Chain of Being, in a pernicious game of "Mother, May I?" As the Reverend James W. C. Pennington, an ex-slave who wrote a slave narrative and who was a prominent black abolitionist, summarized this curious idea in his prefatory note "To the Reader" that authorized Ann Plato's 1841 book of essays, biographies, and poems: "The history of the arts and sciences is the history of individuals, of individual nations." Only by publishing books such as Plato's, he argued, could blacks demonstrate "the fallacy of that stupid theory, *that nature has done nothing but fit us for slaves, and that art cannot unfit us for slavery!*"

IV

The relation between what, for lack of a better term, I shall call the "nonwhite" writer and the French, Portuguese, Spanish, and English languages and literatures manifests itself in at least two ways of interest to theorists of literature and literary history. I am thinking here of what in psychoanalytic criticism is sometimes called "the other," and more especially of this "other" as the subject and object in literature. What I mean by citing these two overworked terms is precisely this: how blacks are figures in literature, and also how blacks *figure*, as it were, literature of their own making.

These two poles of a received opposition have been formed, at least since the early seventeenth century, by an extraordinary *subdiscourse* of the European philosophies of aesthetic theory and language. The two subjects, often in marginal ways, have addressed directly the supposed relation among "race," defined variously as language use and "place in nature." Human beings wrote books. Beautiful books were reflections of sublime genius. Sublime genius was the province of the European.

Blacks, and other people of color, could not "write." "Writing," these writers argued, stood alone among the fine arts as the most salient repository of "genius," the visible sign of reason itself. In this subordinate role, however, "writing," although secondary to "reason," was nevertheless the *medium* of reason's expression. They *knew* reason by its writing, by its representations. This representation could assume the spoken or the written form. And while several superb scholars gave priority to the *spoken* as the privileged of the pair, in their writings about blacks, at least, Europeans privileged *writing* as the principal measure of Africans' "humanity," their "capacity for progress," their very place in "the great chain of being."

This system of signs is arbitrary. Key words, such as *capacity*, which became a metaphor for cranial size, reflect the predominance of "scientific" discourse in metaphysics. That "reason," moreover, could be seen to be "natural" was the key third term of a homology which, in practice, was put to pernicious uses. The transformation of writing from an activity of mind into a commodity not only reflects larger mercantile relations between Africa and Europe but is also the subject I wish to explore here. Let me retrace, in brief, the history of this idea, of the relationship of the absence of "writing" and the absence of "humanity" in European letters of 1600.

We must understand this correlation of use and *presence* in language if we are to begin to learn how to read, for example, the slave's narrative within what Geoffrey H. Hartman calls its "text-milieu." The slave narratives, taken together, represent the attempt of blacks to *write themselves into being*. What a curious idea: Through the mastery of formal Western languages, the presupposition went, a black person could posit a full and sufficient self, as an act of self-creation through the medium of language. Accused of having no collective history by Hegel, blacks effectively responded by publishing hundreds of individual histories which functioned as the part standing for the whole. As Ralph Ellison defined this relation, "We tell ourselves our individual stories so as to become aware of our *general* story."

Writing as the visible sign of Reason, at least since the Renaissance in Europe, had been consistently invoked in Western aesthetic theory in the discussion of the enslavement and status of the black. The origin of this received association of political salvation and artistic genius can be traced at least to the seventeenth century. What we arrive at by extracting a rather black and slender thread from among the philosophical discourses of the Enlightenment is a reading of another side of the philosophy of enlightenment, indeed its nether side. Writing in *The New Organon* in 1620, Sir Francis Bacon, confronted with the problem of classifying the people of color which a seafaring Renaissance Europe had "discovered," turned to the arts as the ultimate measure of a race's place in nature. "Again," he wrote, "let a man only consider what a difference there is between the life of men in the most civilized province of Europe, and in the wildest and most barbarous districts of New India; he will feel it be great enough to justify the saying that 'man is a god to man,' not only in regard to aid and benefit, but also by comparison of condition. And this difference comes not from soil, not from climate, not from race, but from the arts." Eleven years later, Peter Heylyn, in his *Little Description of the Great World,* used Bacon's formulation to relegate the blacks to a subhuman status: Black Africans, he wrote, lacked completely "the use of Reason which is peculiar unto man; [they are] of little Wit; and destitute of all arts and sciences; prone to luxury, and for the greatest part Idolators." All subsequent commentaries on the matter were elaborations upon Heylyn's position.

By 1680, Heylyn's key words, *reason* and *wit,* had been reduced to "reading and writing," as Morgan Godwyn's summary of received opinion attests:

> [A] disingenuous and unmanly *Position* had been formed; and privately (and as it were *in the dark*) handed to and again, which is this, That the Negro's though in their figure they carry some resemblances of manhood, yet are indeed *no* men. . . . the consideration of the shape and figure of our Negro's Bodies, their Limbs and members; their Voice and Countenance, in all things according with other mens; together with their *Risibility* and *Discourse* (man's Peculiar Faculties) should be sufficient Conviction. How should they otherwise be capable of *Trades,* and other no less manly imployments; as also of *Reading and Writing,* or show so much Discretion in management of Business; . . . but wherein (we know) that many of our own People are *deficient,* were they not truly Men?

Such a direct correlation of political rights and literacy helps us to understand both the transformation of writing into a commodity and the sheer burden of received opinion that motivated the black slave to seek his or her text. As well, it defined the "frame" against which each black text would be read. The following 1740 South Carolina Statute was concerned to make it impossible for black literacy mastery even to occur:

And whereas the having of slaves taught to write, or suffering them to be employed in writing, may be attending with great inconveniences;

Be it enacted, that all and every person and persons whatsoever, who shall hereafter teach, or cause any slave or slaves to be taught to write, or shall use or employ any slave as a scribe in any manner of writing whatsoever, hereafter taught to write; every such person or persons shall, for every offense, forfeith the sum of one hundred pounds current money.

Learning to read and to write, then, was not only difficult, it was a violation of a law. That Frederick Douglass, Thomas Smallwood, William Wells Brown, Moses Grandy, James Pennington, and John Thompson, among numerous others, all rendered statements about the direct relation between freedom and discourse not only as central scenes of instruction but also as repeated fundamental structures of their very rhetorical strategies only emphasizes the dialectical relation of black texts to a "context," defined here as "*other*," racist texts, against which the slave's narrative, by definition, was forced to react.

By 1705, a Dutch explorer, William Bosman, had encased Peter Heylyn's bias into a myth which the Africans he had "discovered" had purportedly related to him. It is curious insofar as it justifies human slavery. According to Bosman, the blacks "tell us that in the beginning God created Black as well as White men; thereby giving the Blacks the first Election, who chose Gold, and left the Knowledge of Letters to the White. God granted their request, but being incensed at their Avarice, resolved that the Whites should ever be their masters, and they obliged to wait on them as their slaves." Bosman's fabrication, of course, was a myth of origins designed to sanction through mythology a political order created by Europeans. It was David Hume, writing at midpoint in the eighteenth century, who gave to Bosman's myth the sanction of Enlightenment philosophical reasoning.

In a major essay, "Of National Characters" (1748), Hume discussed the "characteristics" of the world's major division of human beings. In a footnote added to his original text in 1753 (the margins of his discourse), Hume posited with all of the authority of philosophy the fundamental identity of complexion, character, and intellectual capacity. "I am apt to suspect the negroes," he wrote,

> and in general all the other species of men (for there are four or five different kinds) to be naturally inferior to the whites. There never was a civilized nation of any other complexion that white, nor even any individual eminent either in action or speculation. No ingenious manufacturers amongst them, *no arts, no sciences.* . . . Such a uniform and constant difference could not happen, in so many countries and ages, if *nature* had not made our original distinction betwixt these breeds of men. Not to mention our colonies, there are Negroe slaves dispersed all over Europe, of which none ever discovered any symptoms of ingenuity; . . . In Jamaica, indeed they talk of one negroe as a man of parts and learning [Francis Williams, the Cambridge-educated poet who wrote verse in Latin]; but 'tis likely he is admired for very slender accomplishments, like a parrot who speaks a few words plainly.

Hume's opinion on the subject, as we might expect, became prescriptive.

Writing in 1764, in his *Observations on the Feelings of the Beautiful and the Sublime,* Immanuel Kant elaborated upon Hume's essay in a fourth section entitled "Of National Characteristics, as far as They Depend upon the Distinct Feeling of the Beautiful and the Sublime." Kant first claimed that "So fundamental is the difference between [the black and white] races of man, and it appears to be as great in regard to mental capacities as in color." Kant, moreover, was one of the earliest major European philosophers to conflate "color" with "intelligence," a determining relation he posited with dictatorial surety. The excerpt bears citation:

. . . Father Labat reports that a Negro carpenter, whom he reproached for haughty treatment toward his wives, answered: "You whites are indeed fools, for first you make great concessions to your wives, and afterward you complain when they drive you mad." And it might be that there were something in this which perhaps deserved to be considered; but in short, this fellow was *quite black* from head to foot, a clear proof that what he said was stupid. (emphasis added)

The correlation of "blackness" and "stupidity" Kant posited as if self-evident.

Writing in "Query XIV" of *Notes on the State of Virginia*, Thomas Jefferson maintained that "Never yet could I find that a black had uttered a thought above the level of plain narration, never see even an elementary trait of painting or sculpture." Of Wheatley, the first black person to publish a book of poetry in England, Jefferson the critic wrote, "Misery is often the parent of the most affecting touches in poetry. Among the blacks is misery enough, God knows, but not poetry. . . . The compositions published under her name are below the dignity of criticism."

In that same year (1785), Kant, basing his observations on the absence of published writing among blacks, noted as if simply obvious that "Americans [Indians] and blacks are lower in their mental capacities than all other races." Again, Hegel, echoing Hume and Kant, noted the absence of history among black people and derided them for failing to develop indigenous African scripts, or even to master the art of writing in modern languages.

Hegel's strictures on the African about the absence of "history" presume a crucial role of *memory* — a collective, cultural memory — in the estimation of civilization. Metaphors of the "childlike" nature of the slaves, of the masked, puppetlike "personality" of the black, all share this assumption about the absence of memory. Mary Langdon, in her 1855 novel *Ida May: A Story of Things*

Actual and Possible, wrote that "but then they *are* mere children. . . . You seldom hear them say much about anything that's past, if they only get enough to eat and drink at the present moment." Without writing, there could exist no *repeatable* sign of the workings of reason, of mind. Without memory or mind, there could exist no history. Without history, there could exist no "humanity," as defined consistently from Vico to Hegel. As William Gilmore Simms argued at the middle of the nineteenth century:

> [If one can establish] that the negro intellect is fully equal to that of the white race . . . you not only take away the best argument for keeping him in subjection, but you take away the possibility of doing so. *Prima facie,* however, the fact that he *is* a slave, is conclusive against the argument for his freedom, as it is against his equality of claim in respect of intellect. . . . Whenever the negro shall be fully fit for freedom, he will make himself free, and no power on earth can prevent him.

V

Ironically, Anglo-African writing arose as a response to allegations of its absence. Black people responded to these profoundly serious allegations about their "nature" as directly as they could: they wrote books, poetry, autobiographical narratives. Political and philosophical discourse were the predominant forms of writing. Among these, autobiographical "deliverance" narratives were the most common, and the most accomplished. Accused of lacking a formal and collective history, blacks published individual histories which, taken together, were intended to narrate, in segments, the larger yet fragmented history of blacks in Africa, now dispersed throughout a cold New World. The narrated, descriptive "eye" was put into service as a literary form to posit both the individual "I" of the black author and the collective "I" of the race. Text created author, and black authors, it was hoped, would create, or re-create, the image of the race in European discourse. The very *face* of the race, representations of the features of which are common in all sorts of writings about blacks at this time, was contingent upon the recording of the black *voice*. Voice presupposes a face but also seems to have been thought to determine the contours of the black face.

The recording of an "authentic" black voice, a voice of deliverance from the deafening discursive silence which an enlightened Europe cited as proof of the absence of the African's humanity, was the millennial instrument of transformation through which the African would become the European, the slave become the ex-slave, the brute animal become the human being. So central was this idea to the birth of the black literary tradition in the eighteenth century that five of the earliest slave narratives draw upon the figure of the voice in the text as crucial "scenes of instruction" in the development of the slave on the road to freedom. James Gronniosaw in 1770, John Marrant in 1785, Ottobah Cugoano in 1787, Olaudah Equiano in 1789, and John Jea in 1815 — all drew upon the trope of the talking book. Gronniosaw's usage bears citing here especially because it repeats Kant's correlation of physical — and, as it were, metaphysical — characteristics:

> My master used to read prayers in public to the ship's crew every Sabbath day; and when I first saw him read, I was never so surprised in my life, as when I saw the book talk to my master, for I thought it did, as I observed him to look upon it, and move his lips. I wished it would do so with me. As soon as my master had done reading, I followed him to the place where he put the book, being mightily delighted with it, and when nobody saw me, I opened it, and put my ear down close upon it, in great hope that it would say something to me; but I was very sorry, and greatly disap-

> pointed, when I found that it would not speak. This thought
> immediately presented itself to me, that every body and ev-
> ery thing despised me because I was black.

Even for this black author, his own mask of black humanity was a negation, a sign of absence. Gronniosaw accepted his role as a nonspeaking would-be subject and
the absence of his common humanity with the European.

That the figure of the talking book recurs in these
five black eighteenth-century texts says much about the
degree of presupposition and intertextuality in early black
letters, more than we heretofore thought. Equally important, however, this figure itself underscores the received
correlation between silence and blackness which we have
been tracing, as well as the urgent need to make the text
speak, the process by which the slave marked his distance
from the master. The voice in the text was truly a millennial voice for the African person of letters in the eighteenth century, for it was that very voice of deliverance
and of redemption which would signify a new order for
the black.

These narrators, linked by revision of a trope into the
very first black chain of signifiers, implicitly signify upon
another "chain," the metaphorical Great Chain of Being.
Blacks were most commonly represented on the chain
either as the "lowest" of the human races, or as first
cousin to the ape. Since writing, according to Hume,
was the ultimate sign of difference between animal and
human, these writers implicitly were Signifyin(g) upon
the figure of the chain itself, simply by publishing autobi-
ographies that were indictments of the received order of
Western culture, of which slavery, to them, by definition
stood as the most salient sign. The writings of Gronniosaw, Marrant, Equiano, Cugoano, and Jea served as a
critique of the sign of the Chain of Being and the black
person's figurative "place" on the chain. This chain of
black signifiers, regardless of their intent or desire, made

the first political gesture in the Anglo-African literary tradition "simply" by the act of writing, a collective act that gave birth to the black literary tradition and defined it as the "other's chain," the chain of black being as black people themselves would have it. Making the book speak, then, constituted a motivated, and political, engagement with and condemnation of Europe's fundamental figure of domination, the Great Chain of Being.

The trope of the talking book is not a trope of the presence of voice at all, but of its absence. To speak of a "silent voice" is to speak in an oxymoron. There is no such thing as a silent voice. Furthermore, as Juliet Mitchell has put the matter, there is something untenable about the attempt to represent what is not there, to represent that which is *missing* or absent. Given that this is what these five black authors sought to do, we are justified in wondering aloud if the sort of subjectivity that they sought could be realized through a process that was so very ironic from the outset. Indeed, how can the black subject posit a full and sufficient self in a language in which blackness is a sign of absence? Can writing, the very "difference" it makes and marks, mask the blackness of the black face that addresses the text of Western letters, in a voice that "speaks English" in an idiom that contains the irreducible element of cultural difference that shall always separate the white voice from the black? Black people, we know, have not been "liberated" from racism by their writings, and they accepted a false premise by assuming that racism would be destroyed once white racists became convinced that we were human, too. Writing stood as a complex "certificate of humanity," as Paulin J. Hountondji put it. Black writing, and especially the literature of the slave, served not to obliterate the difference of "race," as a would-be white man such as Gronniosaw so ardently desired; rather, the inscription of the black voice in Western literatures has preserved those very cultural differences to be imitated and revised in a separate Western literary tradition, a tradition of black difference.

Blacks, as we have seen, tried to write themselves out of slavery, a slavery even more profound than mere physical bondage. Accepting the challenge of the great white Western tradition, black writers wrote as if their lives depended upon it — and, in a curious sense, their lives did, the "life" of "the race" in Western discourse. But if blacks accepted this challenge, we also accepted its premises, premises in which perhaps lay concealed a trap. What trap might this be? Let us recall the curious case of M. Edmond Laforest.

In 1915, Edmond Laforest, a prominent member of the Haitian literary movement called La Ronde, made of his death a symbolic, if ironic, statement of the curious relation of the "non-Western" writer to the act of writing in a modern language. M. Laforest, with an inimitable, if fatal, flair for the grand gesture, stood upon a bridge, calmly tied a Larousse dictionary around his neck, then proceeded to leap to his death by drowning. While other black writers, before and after M. Laforest, have suffocated as artists beneath the weight of various modern languages, Laforest chose to make his death an emblem of this relation of indenture.

It is the challenge of the black tradition to critique this relation of indenture, an indenture that obtains for our writers and for our critics. We must master, as Derrida wrote, "how to speak the other's language without renouncing (our) own." When we attempt to appropriate, by inversion, *race* as a term for an essence, as did the Negritude movement, for example ("We feel, therefore we are," as Senghor argued of the African), we yield too much, such as the basis of a shared humanity. Such gestures, as Anthony Appiah has observed, are futile, and dangerous because of their further inscription of new and bizarre stereotypes. Who do we meet Derrida's challenge in the discourse of criticism? The Western critical tradition has a canon, just as does the Western literary tradition. Whereas I once thought it our most important gesture to *master* the canon of criticism, to *imitate* and *apply* it, I now believe that we must turn to the black tradition itself to arrive at theories of criticism indigenous to our literatures. Alice Walker's revision of a parable of white interpretation written in 1836 by Rebecca Cox Jackson, a Shaker eldress and black visionary, makes this point most tellingly. Jackson, who like John Jea claimed to have been taught to read by the Lord, wrote in her autobiography that she dreamed that a "white man" came to her house to teach her how to *interpret* and "understand" the word of God, now that God had taught her to read:

> A white man took me by my right hand and led me on the north side of the room, where sat a square table. On it lay a book open. And he said to me. "Thou shall be instructed in this book, from Genesis to Revelations." And then he took me on the west side, where stood a table. And it looked like the first. And said, "Yea, thou shall be instructed from the beginning of creation to the end of time." And then he took me on the east side of the room also, where stood a table and book like the two first, and said, "I will instruct thee — yea, thou shall be instructed from the beginning of all things to the end of all things. Yea, thou shall be well instructed. I will instruct."

> ■   ■   ■

> And then I awoke, and I saw him as plain as I did in my dream. And after that he taught me daily. And when I would be reading and come to a hard word, I would see him standing by my side and he would teach me the word right. And often, when I would be in meditation and looking into things which was hard to understand, I would find him by me, teaching and giving me understanding. And oh, his labor and care which he had with me often caused me to weep bitterly, when I would see my great ignorance and the great

trouble he had to make me understand eternal things. For I
was so buried in the depth of the tradition of my forefathers,
that it did seem as if I never could be dug up.

In response to Jackson's relation of interpretive indenture
to a "white man," Alice Walker, writing in *The Color
Purple,* records and exchange between Celie and Shug
about turning away from "the old white man," which
soon turns into a conversation about the elimination of
"man" as a mediator between a woman and "everything":

> . . . You have to git man off your eyeball, before you can
> see anything a'tall.
> Man corrupt everything, say Shug. He on your box of
> grits, in your head, and all over the radio. He try to make
> you think he everywhere. Soon as you think he everywhere,
> you think he God. But he ain't. Whenever you trying to
> pray, and man plot himself on the other end of it, tell him to
> git lost, say Shug.

Celie and Shug's omnipresent "man," of course, echoes
the black tradition's epithet for the white power structure, "the man."

For non-Western, so-called noncanonical critics, getting the "man off your eyeball" means using the most
sophisticated critical theories and methods generated by
the Western tradition to reappropriate and to define our
own "colonial" discourses. We must use these theories and
methods insofar as these are relevant and applicable to
the study of our own literatures. The danger in doing so,
however, is best put, again by Anthony Appiah in his
definition of what he calls the "Naipaul fallacy": "It is
not necessary to show that African literature is fundamentally the same as European literature in order to
show that it can be treated with the same tools. . . . Nor
should we endorse a more sinister line . . . : the postcolonial legacy which requires us to show that African
literature is worthy of study precisely (but only) because

it is fundamentally the same as European literature." We *must* not, Appiah concludes, "ask the reader to understand Africa by embedding it in European culture."

We must, of course, analyze the ways in which writing relates to "race," how attitudes toward racial differences generate and structure literary texts by us *and* about us; we must determine how critical methods can effectively disclose the traces of racial difference in literature; but we must also understand how certain forms of difference and the *languages* we employ to define those supposed "differences" not only reinforce each other but tend to create and maintain each other. Similarly, and as importantly, we must analyze the language of contemporary criticism itself, recognizing that hermeneutical systems, especially, are not "universal," "color-blind," or "apolitical," or "neutral." Whereas some critics wonder aloud, as Appiah notes, about such matters as whether or not "a structuralist poetics is inapplicable in Africa because structuralism is European," the concern of the "Third World" critic should properly be to understand the ideological subtext which any critical theory reflects and embodies, and what relation this subtext bears to the production of meaning. No critical theory—be that Marxism, feminism, poststructuralism, Nkrumah's consciencism, or whatever—escapes the specificity of value and ideology, no matter how mediated these may be. To attempt to appropriate our own discourses using Western critical theory "uncritically" is to substitute one mode of neocolonialism for another. To begin to do this in my own tradition, theorists have turned to the black vernacular tradition—to paraphrase Rebecca Cox Jackson, to dig into the depths of the tradition of our foreparents—to isolate the signifying black difference through which to theorize about the so-called Discourse of the Other.

CHAPTER
4

Talking Black:
Critical Signs of the Times

For a language acts in diverse ways, upon the spirit
of a people; even as the spirit of a people acts with a
creative and spiritualizing force upon a language.
— ALEXANDER CRUMMELL, 1860

A new vision began gradually to replace the dream
of political power — a powerful movement, the rise
of another ideal to guide the unguided, another pil-
lar of fire by night after a clouded day. It was the
ideal of "book-learning"; the curiosity, born of compulsory ignorance, to know and test the power of
the cabalistic letters of the white man, the longing
to know. Here at last seemed to have been discovered the mountain path to Canaan; longer than the
highway of Emancipation and law, steep and rug-
ged, but straight, leading to heights high enough to
overlook life.
— W.E.B. DU BOIS, 1903

The knowledge which would teach the white world
was Greek to his own flesh and blood. . . . and
he could not articulate the message of another people.
— W.E.B. DU BOIS, 1903

71

Alexander Crummell, a pioneering nineteenth-century Pan-Africanist, statesman, and missionary who spent the bulk of his creative years as an Anglican minister in Liberia, was also a pioneering intellectual and philosopher of language, founding the American Negro Academy in 1897 and serving as the intellectual godfather of W.E.B. Du Bois. For his first annual address as president of the academy, delivered on December 28, 1897, Crummell selected as his topic "The Attitude of the American Mind Toward the Negro Intellect." Given the occasion of the first annual meeting of the great intellectuals of the race, he could not have chosen a more timely or appropriate subject.

Crummell wished to attack, he said, "the denial of intellectuality in the Negro; the assertion that he was not a human being, that he did not belong to the human race." He argued that the desire "to becloud and stamp out the intellect of the Negro" had led to the enactment of "laws and Statutes, closing the pages of every book printed to the eyes of Negroes; barring the doors of every school-room against them!" This, he concluded, "was the systematized method of the intellect of the South, to stamp out the brains of the Negro!" — a program that created an "almost Egyptian darkness [which] fell upon the mind of the race, throughout the whole land."

Crummell next shared with his audience a conversation between two Boston lawyers which he had overheard when he was "an errand boy in the Anti-slavery office in New York City" in 1833 or 1834:

> While at the Capitol they happened to dine in the company of the great John C. Calhoun, then senator from South Carolina. It was a period of great ferment upon the question of Slavery, States' Rights, and Nullification; and consequently the Negro was the topic of conversation at the table. One of the utterances of Mr. Calhoun was to this effect — "That if he could find a Negro who knew the Greek syntax,

he would then believe that the Negro was a human being and should be treated as a man."

"Just think of the crude asininity," Crummell concluded rather generously, "of even a great man!"

The salient sign of the black person's humanity — indeed, the only sign for Calhoun — would be the mastering of the very essence of Western civilization, of the very foundation of the complex fiction upon which white Western culture had been constructed. It is likely that "Greek syntax," for John C. Calhoun, was merely a hyperbolic figure of speech, a trope of virtual impossibility; he felt driven to the hyperbolic mode, perhaps, because of the long racist tradition in Western letters of demanding that black people *prove* their full humanity. We know this tradition all too well, dotted as it is with the names of the great intellectual Western racialists, such as Francis Bacon, David Hume, Immanuel Kant, Thomas Jefferson, and G.W.F. Hegel. Whereas each of these figures demanded that blacks write poetry to prove their humanity, Calhoun — writing in a post–Phillis Wheatley era — took refuge in, yes, Greek syntax.

In typical African-American fashion, a brilliant black intellectual accepted Calhoun's challenge. The anecdote Crummell shared with his fellow black academicians turned out to be his shaping scene of instruction. For Crummell himself jumped on a boat, sailed to England, and matriculated at Queens' College, Cambridge, where he mastered the intricacies of Greek syntax. Calhoun, we suspect, was not impressed.

Crummell never stopped believing that mastering the master's tongue was the sole path to civilization, intellectual freedom, and social equality for the black person. It was Western "culture," he insisted, that the black person "must claim as his rightful heritage, as a man — not stinted training, not a caste education, not," he concluded

prophetically, "a Negro curriculum." As he argued so passionately in his speech of 1860, "The English Language
in Liberia," the acquisition of the English language,
along with Christianity, is the wonderful sign of God's
providence encoded in the nightmare of African enslavement in the racist wilderness of the New World. English,
for Crummell, was "the speech of Chaucer and Shakespeare, of Milton and Wordsworth, of Bacon and Burke,
of Franklin and Webster," and its potential mastery was
"this one item of compensation" that "the Almighty has
bestowed upon us" in exchange for "the exile of our fa-
thers from their African homes to America." In the English language are embodied "the noblest theories of lib-
erty" and "the grandest ideas of humanity." If black
people master the master's tongue, these great and grand
ideas will become African ideas, because "ideas conserve
men, and keep alive the vitality of nations."

In dark contrast to the splendors of the English language, Crummell set the African vernacular languages,
which, he wrote, have "definite marks of inferiority connected with them all, which place them at the widest
distances from civilized languages." Any effort to render
the master's discourse in our own black tongue is an egre-
gious error, for we cannot translate sublime utterances
"in[to] broken English—a miserable caricature of their
noble tongue." We must abandon forever both indigenous African vernacular languages and the neo-African
vernacular languages that our people have produced in
the New World:

> All low, inferior, and barbarous tongues are, doubtless, but
> the lees and dregs of noble languages, which have gradually,
> as the soul of a nation has died out, sunk down to degrada-
> tion and ruin. We must not suffer this decay on these shores,
> in this nation. We have been made, providentially, the
> deposit of a noble trust; and we should be proud to show
> our appreciation of it. Having come to the heritage of this

language we must cherish its spirit, as well as retain its letter. We must cultivate it among ourselves; we must strive to infuse its spirit among our reclaimed and aspiring natives.

I cite the examples of John C. Calhoun and Alexander Crummell as metaphors for the relation between the critic of black writing and the broader, larger institution of literature. Learning the master's tongue, for our generation of critics, has been an act of empowerment, whether that tongue be New Criticism, humanism, structuralism, Marxism, poststructualism, feminism, new historicism, or any other "ism." Each of these critical discourses arises from a specific set of texts within the Western tradition. At least for the past decade, many of us have busied ourselves with the necessary task of learning about these movements in criticism, drawing upon their modes of reading to explicate the texts in our own tradition.

This is an exciting time for critics of Afro-American literature. More critical essays and books are being produced than ever before, and there have never been more jobs available teaching Afro-American literature in white colleges and universities. In a few years, we shall at last have our very own Norton anthology, a sure sign that the teaching of Afro-American literature is being institutionalized. Our pressing question now becomes this: In what languages shall we choose to speak, and write, our own criticisms? What are we now to do with the enabling masks of empowerment that we have donned as we have practiced one mode of formal criticism or another?

There is a long history of resistance to (white) theory in the (black) tradition. Unlike almost every other, the Afro-American literary tradition was generated as a response to allegations that its authors did not, and *could not* create literature, considered the signal measure of a race's innate "humanity." The African living in Europe

or in the New World seems to have felt compelled to
create a literature not only to demonstrate that blacks did
indeed possess the intellectual ability to create a written
art, but also to indict the several social and economic
institutions that delimited the "humanity" of all black
people in Western cultures.

So insistent did these racist allegations prove to be, at
least from the eighteenth to the early twentieth century,
that it is fair to describe the subtext of the history of black
letters in terms of the urge to refute them. Even as late
as 1911, when J. E. Casely-Hayford published *Ethiopia
Unbound* (the "first" African novel), he felt it necessary
to address this matter in the first two paragraphs of this
text. "At the dawn of the twentieth century," the novel
opens, "men of light and leading both in Europe and in
America had not yet made up their minds as to what
place to assign to the spiritual aspirations of the black
man." Few literary traditions have begun with such a
complex and curious relation to criticism: allegations of
an absence led directly to a presence, a literature often
inextricably bound in a dialogue with its harshest critics.

Black literature and its criticism, then, have been put
to uses that were not primarily aesthetic; rather, they
have formed part of a larger discourse on the nature of
the black, and of his or her role in the order of things.
The relation among theory, tradition, and integrity
within black culture has not been, and perhaps cannot
be, a straightforward matter.

Despite the fact that critics of black literature are
often attacked for using theory and that some black readers respond to their work by remarking that it's all Greek
to them, it is probably true that critics of Afro-American
literature are more concerned with the complex relation
between literature and theory than ever before. There
are many reasons for this, not the least of which is our

increasingly central role in "the profession" precisely when our colleagues are engulfed in their own extensive debates about the intellectual merit of so much theorizing. Theory, as a second-order reflection upon a primary gesture, has *always* been viewed with suspicion by scholars who find it presumptuous and even decadent when criticism claims the right to stand on its own: theoretical texts breed equally "decadent" theoretical responses in a creative process that can be very far removed from a poem or a novel.

For the critic of Afro-American literature, this process is even more perilous because most of the contemporary literary theory derives from critics of Western European languages and literatures. Is the use of theory to write about Afro-American literature merely another form of intellectual indenture, a mental servitude as pernicious in its intellectual implications as any other kind of enslavement? The key word implied in this panel discussion is *integrity*. To quote the *Oxford English Dictionary*'s definition of the word, does theorizing about a text or a literary tradition "mar," "violate," "impair," or "corrupt" the "soundness" of an "original perfect state" of a black text or of the black tradition? To argue that it does is to align oneself with the New Critics — who often seem not to have cared particularly for, or about, the writing of Afro-Americans — and with their view that texts are "organic wholes" in the first place. This is a critical error.

The sense of "integrity" as it seems to arise in the Afro-American tradition is more akin to the notion of "ringing true," or to Houston Baker's concept of "sounding." (One of the most frequently used critical judgments in the African-American tradition is "That just don't sound right," or, as Alice Walker puts it in *The Color Purple*, "Look like to me only a fool would want to talk in a way that feel peculiar to your mind.") That is the

sense that black nationalists call on here, without understanding how problematic this can be. Doubleness, alienation, equivocality — since the turn of the century at least,
these have been recurrent tropes for the black tradition.

To be sure, this matter of criticism and "integrity" has
a long and rather tortured history in black letters. It was
David Hume, after all, who called Francis Williams, the
Jamaican poet of Latin verse, "a parrot who merely
speaks a few words plainly." Phillis Wheatley, too, has
long suffered from the spurious attacks of black and white
critics alike for being the *rara avis* of a school of so-called
mockingbird poets, whose use of European and American
literary conventions has been considered a corruption of
a "purer" black expression, found in forms such as the
blues, signifying, spirituals, and Afro-American dance.
Can we, as critics, escape a "mockingbird" relation to
theory? And can we escape the racism of so many critical
theorists, from Hume and Kant through the Southern
Agrarians and the Frankfurt School?

Only recently have some scholars attempted to con-
vince critics of black literature that we can. Perhaps pre-
dictably, a number of these attempts share a concern
with that which has been most repressed in the received
tradition of Afro-American criticism: close readings of
the texts themselves. My advocacy of theory's value for
such readings is meant as a prelude to the definition of
critical principles peculiar to the black literary traditions,
related to contemporary theory generally and yet, as Robert Farris Thompson puts it, "indelibly black." I have
tried to work through contemporary theories of literature
not to "apply" them to black texts, but to transform by
translating them into a new rhetorical realm — to re-
create, through revision, the critical theory at hand. As
our familiarity with the black tradition and with literary
theory expands, we shall invent our own black, text-

specific theories, as some of us have begun to do. We must learn to read a black text within a black formal cultural matrix, as well as its "white" matrix.

This is necessary because the existence of a black canon is a historically contingent phenomenon; it is not inherent in the nature of "blackness," not vouchsafed by the metaphysics of some racial essence. The black tradition exists only insofar as black artists enact it. Only because black writers have read and responded to other black writers with a sense of recognition and acknowledgment can we speak of a black literary inheritance, with all the burdens and ironies that has entailed. Race is a text (an array of discursive practices), not an essence. It must be *read* with painstaking care and suspicion, not imbibed.

I have tried to employ contemporary theory to defamiliarize the texts of the black tradition: ironically, it is necessary to create distance between reader and texts in order to go beyond reflexive responses and achieve critical insight into and intimacy with their formal workings. I have done this to respect the "integrity" of these texts, by trying to avoid confusing my experience as an Afro-American with the act of language that defines a black text. This is the challenge of the critic of black literature in the 1980s: not to shy away from white power — that is, literary theory — but to translate it into the black idiom, *renaming* principles of criticism where appropriate, but especially *naming* indigenous black principles of criticism and applying them to our own texts. *Any* tool that enables the critic to explain the complex workings of the language of a text is appropriate here. For it is language, the black language of black texts, that expresses the distinctive quality of our literary tradition. Once it may have seemed that the only critical implements black critics needed were the pom-pom and the twirled baton; in fact, there

is no deeper form of literary disrespect. We will not pro-
tect the "integrity" of our tradition by remaining afraid
of, or naive about, literary theory; rather, we will inflict
upon it the violation of reflexive, stereotypical readings —
or nonreading. We are the keepers of the black literary
tradition. No matter what theories we embrace, we have
more in common with each other than we do with any
other critic of any other literature. We write for each
other, and for our own contemporary writers. This relations is a critical trust.

It is also a *political* trust. How can the demonstration
that our texts sustain ever closer and more sophisticated
readings *not* be political at a time when all sorts of so-
called canonical critics mediate their racism through calls
for "purity" of the "tradition," demands as implicitly racist as anything the Southern Agrarians said? How can the
deconstruction of the forms of racism itself not be political? How can the use of literary analysis to explicate the
racist social text in which we still find ourselves be anything *but* political? To be political, however, does not
mean that I have to write at the level of a Marvel comic
book. My task, as I see it, is to help guarantee that black
and so-called Third World literature is taught to black
and Third World and white students by black and Third
World and white professors in heretofore white mainstream departments of literature, and to train students to
think, to read, and to write clearly, to expose false uses
of language, fraudulent claims, and muddled arguments,
propaganda, and vicious lies — from all of which our people have suffered just as surely as we have from an economic order in which we were zeros and a metaphysical
order in which we were absences. These are the "values"
which should be transmitted through critical theory.

In the December 1986 issue of the *Voice Literary Supplement,* in an essay entitled "Cult-Nats Meet Freaky-
Deke," Greg Tate argued cogently and compellingly that

"black aestheticians need to develop a coherent criticism to communicate the complexities of our culture. There's no periodical on black cultural phenomena equivalent to *The Village Voice* or *Artforum,* no publication that provides journalism on black visual art, philosophy, politics, economics, media, literature, linguistics, psychology, sexuality, spirituality, and pop culture. Though there are certainly black editors, journalists, and academics capable of producing such a journal, the disentregration of the black cultural nationalist movement and the braindrain of black intellectuals to white institutions have destroyed the vociferous public dialogue that used to exist between them." While I would argue that *Sage, Callaloo,* and *Black American Literature Forum (BALF)* are indeed fulfilling that function for academic critics, I am afraid that the truth of Tate's claim is irresistible.

But his most important contribution to the future of black criticism is to be found in his most damning allegation. "What's unfortunate," he writes, "is that while black artists have opened up the entire 'text of blackness' for fun and games, not many black critics have produced writing as fecund, eclectic, and freaky-deke as the art, let alone the culture, itself. . . . For those who prefer exegesis with a polemical bent, just imagine how critics as fluent in black and Western culture as the postliberated artists could strike terror into that bastion of white supremacist thinking, the Western art [and literary] world[s]." To which I can only say, echoing Shug in Alice Walker's *The Color Purple,* "Amen. Amen."

Tate's challenge is a serious one because neither ideology nor criticism nor blackness can exist as entities of themselves, outside the forms of their texts. This is the central theme of Ralph Ellison's *Invisible Man* and Ishmael Reed's *Mumbo Jumbo,* for example. But how can we write or read the text of "Black Theory"? What language(s) do black people use to represent their critical or

ideological positions? In what forms of language do we
speak or write? Can we derive a valid, integral "black"
text or criticism or ideology from borrowed or appropriate forms? Can a black woman's text emerge "authen-
tically" as borrowed, or "liberated," or revised, from the
patriarchal forms of the slave narratives, on the one
hand, or from the white matriarchal forms of the sentimental novel, on the other, as Harriet Jacobs and Harriet
Wilson attempted to do in *Incidents in the Life of a Slave
Girl* (1861) and *Our Nig* (1859)? Where lies the liberation
in revision, the ideological integrity of defining freedom
in the modes and forms of difference charted so cogently
by so many poststructural critics of black literature?

For it is in these spaces of difference that black literature has dwelled. And while it is crucial to read these
patterns of difference closely, we must understand as well
that the quest was lost, in a major sense, before it had
even begun, simply because the terms of our own self-
representation have been provided by the master. It is
not enough for us to show that refutation, negation, and
revision exist, and to define them as satisfactory gestures
of ideological independence. Our next concern must be
to address the black political signified, that is, the cultural vision and the critical language that underpin the
search through literature and art for a profound re-
ordering and humanizing of everyday existence. We must
urge our writers and critics to undertake the fullest and
most ironic exploration of the manner and matter, the
content and form, the structure and sensibility so familiar
and poignant to us in our most sublime form of art, black
music, where ideology and art are one, whether we listen
to Bessie Smith or to postmodern and poststructural John
Coltrane.

Just as we must urge our writers to meet this challenge, we as critics must turn to our own peculiarly black
structures of thought and feeling to develop our own lan-

guages of criticism. We must do so by drawing on the black vernacular, the language we use to speak to each other when no outsiders are around. Unless we look to the vernacular to ground our theories and modes of reading, we will surely sink in the mire of Nella Larsen's quicksand, remain alienated in the isolation of Harriet Jacob's garret, or masked in the received stereotype of the Black Other helping Huck to return to the raft, singing "China Gate" with Nat King Cole under the Da Nang moon, or reflecting our bald heads in the shining flash of Mr. T's signifying gold chains.

We must redefine theory itself from within our own black cultures, refusing to grant the racist premise that theory is something that white people do, so that we are doomed to imitate our white colleagues, like reverse black minstrel critics done up in whiteface. We are all heirs to critical theory, but critics are also heir to the black vernacular critical tradition as well. We must not succumb, as did Alexander Crummell, to the tragic lure of white power, the mistake of accepting the empowering language of white critical theory as "universal" or as our only language, the mistake of confusing the enabling mask of theory with our own black faces. Each of us has, in some literal or figurative manner, boarded a ship and sailed to a metaphorical Cambridge, seeking to master the master's tools. (I myself, being quite literal-minded, booked passage some fourteen years ago on the *QE2*.) Now we must at last don the empowering mask of blackness and talk *that* talk, the language of black difference. While it is true that we must, as Du Bois said so long ago, "know and test the power of the cabalistic letters of the white man," we must also know and test the dark secrets of a black discursive universe that awaits its disclosure through the black arts of interpretation. For the future of theory, in the remainder of this century, is black indeed.

II

THE
PROFESSION

CHAPTER
5

"Tell Me, Sir, . . . What *Is* 'Black' Literature?"

In memory of James A. Snead

. . . even today, it seems to me (possibly because I am black) very dangerous to model one's opposition to the arbitrary definition, the imposed ordeal, merely on the example supplied by one's oppressor.

The object of one's hatred is never, alas, conveniently outside but is seated in one's lap, stirring in one's bowels and dictating the beat of one's heart. And if one does not know this, one risks becoming an imitation—and, therefore, a continuation—of principles one imagines oneself to despise.

— JAMES BALDWIN, "Here Be Dragons"

For those of us who were students or professors of African or African-American literature in the late sixties or through the seventies, it is a thing of wonder to behold the various ways in which our specialties and the works we explicate and teach have moved, if not exactly from the margins to the center of the profession of literature, at least from defensive postures to a position of generally accepted validity. My own graduate students often greet with polite skepticism an anecdote I draw on in the introduction to my seminars. When I was a student at the University of Cambridge, Wole Soyinka, recently released from a two-year confinement in a Nigerian prison, was on campus to deliver a lecture series on African literature (collected and published by Cambridge in 1976 under the title *Myth, Literature, and the African World*). Soyinka had come to Cambridge in 1973 from Ghana, where he had been living in exile, ostensibly to assume a two-year lectureship in the faculty of English. To his astonishment, as he told me in our first supervision, the faculty of English apparently did not recognize African literature as a legitimate area of study within the "English" tripos, so he had been forced to accept an appointment in social anthropology, of all things! (Much later, the distinguished Nigerian literary scholar Emmanuel Obiechina related a similar tale when I asked him why he had taken his Cambridge doctorate in social anthropology.) Shortly after I heard Soyinka's story, I asked the tutor in English at Clare College, Cambridge, why Soyinka had been treated this way, explaining as politely as I could that I would very much like to write a doctoral thesis on "black literature." To which the tutor replied with great disdain, "Tell me, sir, . . . what *is* black literature?" When I responded with a veritable bibliography of texts written by authors who were black, his evident irritation informed me that I had taken as a serious request for information what he had intended as a rhetorical question.

Few, if any, students or scholars of African or African-American literature encounter the sort of hostility, skepticism, or suspicion that Soyinka, Obiechina, and I did at the University of Cambridge. (To be perfectly fair, I should add that I was later able to find professors who, confessing their ignorance of my topic, were quite willing to allow me to work with them and to write the Ph.D. thesis I chose. The faculty of English there is even trying to fund a chair in "Commonwealth Literature.") At Oxford, meanwhile, a scholar of African-American literature is to deliver the Clarendon Lectures in the spring of 1992. At Oxford, Cambridge, Sussex, Birmingham, and Kent—to list just a few institutions—sophisticated and innovative work in "postcolonial" literary criticism is defining this branch of study. Many of the youngest scholars in the field are accepting teaching positions in Africa, India, Pakistan, and throughout the "Third World," attempting to wrestle control of pedagogy and scholarship from older conservative scholars, who are still under the spell of F. R. Leavis (whose influence on "Third World" literary pedagogy merits several doctoral dissertations) and who still believe in the possibility of a "pretheoretical" practical criticism.

In the United States, the status of black literatures within the academy has changed even more dramatically. Since 1985, according to the *MLA Job Information Lists*, few departments of English, for example, have not engaged in, or will not continue to engage in, searches for junior and senior professors of African-American, African, or postcolonial literatures. Because of the sharp increase in demand, along with the scarcity of Ph.D.'s in these fields, scholars of African-American literature commonly find themselves pursued by several departments competing to make imaginative job offers—especially at institutions that confuse the inclusion of black studies with affirmative action. Although nonminority job seekers in this area sometimes encounter difficulties reaching, or surviving, interviews at the MLA convention (if their ethnic identities have not been ascertained beforehand, often by phone calls to their referees) several of the major scholar-critics of African-American and African literature are white. (Last year, I wrote *forty-nine* letters of recommendation for one talented white job candidate in African literature; all forty-nine applications were unsuccessful.) Despite such exceptional instances, however, African-American and African literatures have never been more widely taught or analyzed in the academy than they are today. We have come a long way since the early twenties, when Charles Eaton Burch (1891–1941), as chairman of the department of English at Howard, introduced into the curriculum a course entitled Poetry and Prose of Negro Life, and a long way, too, from the mid-thirties, when James Weldon Johnson, then the Adam K. Spence Professor of Creative Literature and Writing at Fisk University, became the first scholar to teach black literature at a white institution, New York University, where he delivered an annual lecture series on "Negro Literature."

These larger changes, however, have yet to reach the high schools. As Arthur N. Applebee reports, Shakespeare, Steinbeck, Dickens, and Twain are the most frequently required authors, even in public schools with the highest proportion of minority students. In public schools overall, only Lorraine Hansberry and Richard Wright appear among the top fifty authors required in English classes between grades 7 and 12. In urban schools they rank twenty-fifth and thirty-seventh. In schools with a 50 percent or higher minority enrollment, they rank only fourteenth and seventeenth (p. 16). (Wright's *Black Boy*, in contrast, is among the three books most frequently banned from public schools.) These figures are still more surprising when we recall the extraordinarily large sales of the novels of Toni Morrison, Alice Walker, and Gloria

Naylor. Clearly the opening of the canon in traditional university literature departments has not yet affected the pedagogical practices of high school teachers.

What has happened within the profession of literature at the college level to elevate the status of African-American and other "minority" texts within the past decade and a half? It is difficult to be certain about the reasons for the heightened popularity of any area of study. Nevertheless, we can isolate several factors that, in retrospect, seem to bear directly both on the growth of student interest in these fields — an interest that has never been greater, if we can judge from the proliferation of titles being produced and the high sales figures — and on the vast increase in the number of teachers attempting to satisfy student demand.

One factor would seem to be the women's movement within African-American and African literature. Since 1970, when Toni Morrison published *The Bluest Eye*, Alice Walker published *The Third Life of Grange Copeland*, and Toni Cade Bambara published her anthology, *The Black Woman*, black women writers have produced a remarkable number of novels and books of poetry. Morrison alone has published five novels, Walker four, and Gloria Naylor three. The list of black women writers with first and second novels is a very long one. Walker, Morrison, Naylor, and, in poetry, Rita Dove have won Pulitzer Prizes and National and American Book Awards; before 1970, Ralph Ellison and Gwendolyn Brooks were the only black writers who had been accorded these honors. The works by black women novelists, especially Walker and Morrison, are selling in record-breaking numbers, in part because of an expanded market that includes white and black feminists as well as the general black studies readership. What has happened, clearly, is that the feminist movement, in the form of women's studies on campus and the abandonment of quotas for the admission of women to heretofore elite male institutions, has had a direct impact on what we might think of as black women's studies. Indeed, black studies and women's studies have met on the common terrain of black women's studies, ensuring a larger audience for black women authors than ever before.

Scholars of women's studies have accepted the work and lives of black women as their subject matter in a manner unprecedented in the American academy. Perhaps only the Anglo-American abolitionist movement was as cosmopolitan as the women's movement has been in its concern for the literature of blacks. Certainly, Richard Wright, Ralph Ellison, and James Baldwin did not become the subjects of essays, reviews, books, and dissertations as quickly as Morrison and Walker have. Hurston, of course, attracted her largest following only after 1975, precisely when other black women authors rose to prominence. The women's studies movement in the academy has given new life to African-American studies, broadly conceived.

Forecasts of the death of African-American studies abounded in 1975. Although the field had benefited from a great burst of interest in the late sixties, when student protests on its behalf were at their noisiest, it had begun to stagnate by the mid-seventies, as many ill-conceived, politically overt programs collapsed or were relegated to an even more marginal status than they had had before. American publishers, ever sensitive to their own predictions about market size, became reluctant to publish works in this field. Toni Morrison, however, herself an editor at Random House, continued to publish texts by black women and men, from Africa, the Caribbean, and the United States. The burgeoning sales of books by black women, for many of whom Morrison served as editor, began to reverse the trends that by 1975 had jeopardized the survival of black studies. Morrison's own novels, especially *Tar Baby* (1981), which led to a cover story in *Newsweek*, were pivotal in redefining the market for books in black studies. The popularity of — and the controversy surrounding — Michele Wallace's *Black Macho and the Myth of the Superwoman* (1978) and Ntozake Shange's *For Coloured Girls Who Have Considered Suicide* (1977) also generated a great amount of interest in the writings of black women.

Simultaneously, within the academy, scholars of black literature were undertaking important projects that would bear directly on the direction of their field. Whereas in the late sixties, when black studies formally entered the curriculum, history had been the predominant subject, a decade later, literary studies had become the "glamor" area of black studies. While the black arts movement of the mid-sixties had declared literature, and especially poetry, to be the cultural wing of the black power revolution, it had little effect on the curricula offered by traditional departments of English. As Kimberly Benston aptly characterizes the import of this movement, "the profound reorientation of energy and vision which took place among Afro-American thinkers, writers, performers, and their audiences during this period, centering on considerations of a nationalist, or *sui generis*, understanding of the 'black self,' took place through dynamic and complex *disputations* about the provenance, nature, and teleology of the sign of blackness." More than any other single factor, the black arts movement gave birth to the larger black studies movement, even if it did not have a direct impact on traditional university literature departments. This intervention would be dependent on the studies produced by a group of younger scholars — Donald Gibson, June Jordan, Houston A. Baker, Jr., Robert Stepto, Arnold Rampersad, Geneva Smitherman, Jerry Ward, Mary Helen Washington, Kimberly Benston,

Addison Gayle, Werner Sollors, Stephen Henderson, Sherley Ann Williams, Carolyn Fowler, R. Baxter Miller, and others — many of whom had been trained by an older generation of African-Americanists. That generation included such literary critics as Charles Davis, Charles Nilon, Michael G. Cooke, Margaret Walker, Charles Nichols, Richard Barksdale, Blyden Jackson, Darwin Turner, and J. Saunders Redding, many of whom had been recruited to previously segregated schools in response to student demands for the creation of black studies, as well as Arthur P. Davis, Hugh Gloster, Sterling Brown, and others who remained at historically black colleges.

For a variety of reasons, and in a remarkable variety of ways, these scholars began to theorize about the nature and function of black literature and its criticism and, simultaneously, to train an even younger generation of students. While it is difficult, precisely, to characterize their concerns, it seems safe to say that they shared a concern with the "literariness" of African-American works, as they wrestled to make these texts a "proper" object of analysis within traditional departments of English. Whereas black literature had generally been taught and analyzed through an interdisciplinary methodology, in which sociology and history (and, for African literature, anthropology) had virtually blocked out the "literariness" of the black text, these scholars, after 1975, began to argue for the explication of the formal properties of the writing. If the "blackness" of a text was to be found anywhere, they argued, it would be in the practical uses of language. So, at a time when theorists of European and Anglo-American literature were offering critiques of Anglo-American formalism, scholars of black literature, responding to the history of their own discipline, found it "radical" to teach formal methods of reading.

Of the several gestures that were of great importance

to this movement, I can mention only three here. In chronological order, these are Dexter Fisher's *Minority Language and Literature* (1977), Dexter Fisher and Robert Stepto's *Afro-American Literature: The Reconstruction of Instruction* (1979), and Leslie Fiedler and Houston A. Baker, Jr.'s *Opening Up the Canon: Selected Papers from the English Institute, 1979* (1981). Conveniently, for my argument here, each of these anthologies, the published results of seminal conferences, expresses a different aspect of a larger movement.

The first two collections grew out of conferences sponsored by the Modern Language Association (MLA), while the third was sponsored by the English Institute. "In an effort to address the critical, philosophical, pedagogical, and curricular issues surrounding the teaching of minority literature," Dexter Fisher explains in her introduction to *Minority Language and Literature*, the MLA in 1972 formed the Commission on Minority Groups and the Study of Language and Literature. (Until the early seventies, black scholars did not find the MLA a welcoming institution; they formed instead the predominantly black College Language Association, which still thrives today. The commission's establishment was an attempt, in part, to redefine the MLA sufficiently to "open up" its membership to black and other minority professors.) Beginning in 1974, the commission, funded by the National Endowment for the Humanities (NEH), sponsored various colloquiums "to stimulate greater awareness and to encourage more equitable representation of minority literature in the mainstream of literary studies" (8). Fisher's book stemmed directly from a conference held in 1976, at which forty-four scholars, publishers, and foundation program officers came together to consider "the relationship of minority literature to the mainstream of American literary tradition":

One of the major issues raised repeatedly at Commission-sponsored meetings is the relationship of minority literature to the mainstream of American literary tradition. The question of the "place" of minority literature in American literature raises a deeper, and perhaps more controversial, question: "In what ways does minority literature share the values and assumptions of the dominant culture, and in what ways does it express divergent perspectives?" This question has implications not only for curriculum development and critical theory, but also, and even more important, for the role of the humanities in bringing about a truly plural system of education.   (9)

The conference's participants, including J. Lee Greene, Mary Helen Washington, Michael G. Cooke, Michael Harper, Geneva Smitherman, and Houston A. Baker, Jr., each a specialist in African-American literature, explored the relations between "principles of criticism" and social contexts. As Fisher puts it nicely:

The emergence of the Black Aesthetics Movement in the 1960s focused attention on the dilemma faced by minority writers trying to reconcile cultural dualism. Willingly or otherwise, minority writers inherit certain tenets of Western civilization through American society, though they often live alienated from that society. At the same time, they may write out of a cultural and linguistic tradition that sharply departs from the mainstream. Not only does this present constant social, political, and literary choices to minority writers, but it also challenges certain aesthetic principles of evaluation for the critic. When the cultural gap between writer and critic is too great, new critical approaches are needed.   (11)

Above all else, the conference was concerned with "revising the canons of American literature," a matter that Fiedler and Baker would explore in even broader terms three years later at the English Institute.

In the same year that Fisher's volume appeared, she

and Robert Stepto, a professor of English, American, and
Afro-American studies at Yale, again with NEH funding,
convened a two-week seminar at Yale entitled Afro-
American Literature: From Critical Approach to Course
Design. The five seminar leaders — Fisher, Stepto, Robert
O'Meally, Sherley Anne Williams, and I — defined its
purpose as "the reconstruction of instruction": "in this
case," as Fisher and Stepto put it, "to design courses in,
and to refine critical approaches to, Afro-American literature yielding a 'literary' understanding of the literature"
(vii). The "literary," Stepto explains, is contrasted with
the "sociological," the "ideological, etc." Noting that
"many schools still do not teach Afro-American literature, while other institutions offering courses in the field
seem to be caught in a lockstep of stale critical and pedagogical ideas, many of which are tattered hand-me-
downs from disciplines other than literature" (1), Stepto
and his colleagues, with all the zeal of reformers, sought
to redefine African-American literary study by introducing into its explication formalist and structuralist methods
of reading and by providing a critique of the essentialism
of black aesthetic criticism that had grown out of the
black arts movement. These scholars were intent on defining a canon of both African-American literature and
its attendant formal critical practices.

As bold and as controversial as the Fisher–Stepto volume was within African-American literary studies, the
volume edited by Fiedler and Baker was perhaps even
more daring, since it sought to explode the notion that
English is, somehow — or could ever be, somehow — a
neutral container for "world literature." Indeed, the institute's theme in 1979 was English as a World Language
for Literature. The volume, featuring papers by Dennis
Brutus and Edward Kamau Braithwaite on South African
and Caribbean literature, respectively, carries a succinct
yet seminal introduction by Baker that suggests some-

thing of the polemics generated by the notion that English might be anything but the most fertile and flexible language available to any writer for the fullest expression of literary sensibility. Baker's laconic remarks, made just a decade ago, suggest the heated responses of the institute's audiences to the participants' critique of the "neocolonialism" of traditional English studies and to Baker's observations that "the conception of English as a 'world language' is rooted in Western economic history" and that we must juxtapose "the economic ascendancy of English and the historical correlation between this academy and processes of modern thought." English literature, Baker concludes, is not what it appears to be:

> The fact that a Sotho writer claims that he has chosen English because it guarantees a wide audience and ensures access to the literary reproduction systems of a world market may be less important as a literary consideration than what the writer has actually made of the English language as a literary agency. One might want to ask, for example, what summits of experience inaccessible to occupants of the heartland have been incorporated into the world of English literature? What literary strategies have been employed by the Sotho writer to preserve and communicate culturally-specific meanings? What codes of analysis and evaluation must be articulated in order to render accurate explanations for a Sotho or a Tewa or a Yoruba literary work written in English? (xiii)

These foundational volumes proved to be, each in its own way, enabling gestures for the growth of sophisticated theories and critical practices in African, Caribbean, and African-American literatures. In the past decade, scores of books and hundreds of essays, reflecting structuralists, poststructuralist, gay, lesbian, Marxist, and feminist theories and practices, have been devoted to the study of black literature. Even the essentialism of race itself, long thought to be a sacrosanct concept within

African-American studies, has been extensively analyzed as a social construction rather than a thing. The black women's literary renaissance has found counterparts in Africa and the Caribbean. Since 1970 alone, fifty-six novels by black women have been published in the Caribbean. One scholar even declared recently that we are living in the age of the greatest African-American novelist (Morrison). Therefore the critical endeavor in black literary studies has a certain immediacy not found in other English studies. Derek Walcott's achievements in poetry and Soyinka's in the drama have had a similar effect on the study of Caribbean and African literature. That this generation of critics lives contemporaneously with the first black Nobel laureate is only one sign, albeit a large one, of the vibrancy and youth of the field today.

When the MLA's Executive Council and *PMLA*'s Editorial Board decided to introduce "special topics" into *PMLA*'s format, the unanimous choice for the first issue was African and African-American literature. Despite the great activity in the field, the journal had published only three essays in this area. And despite the large number of sessions devoted to such topics at the annual convention, membership in the African, black American, and ethnic divisions remained surprisingly low. While the black American division had grown by a remarkable 93.3 percent between 1985 and 1987, there were still only 319 members. We hoped that our announcement of this special topic would attract new members to these divisions.

We were not to be disappointed. Since 1987, when the first advertisement for this special topic appeared, memberships in the three divisions have grown dramatically.

And what is the current state of the field? While one can be encouraged by the important institutional interventions that are serving to integrate African and African-American literature into traditional literature departments and by the several editorial ventures that are making "lost" black texts available once again and generating sophisticated reference works and anthologies, black authors are still not well represented in many college curricula. (It is one of the paradoxes of pedagogic reform that the newfound prominence of black literature is still primarily a phenomenon of elite institutions.) Moreover, a large percentage of those who teach this literature are black, and such black scholars are themselves a diminishing presence in the profession. (In 1986, according to the National Research Council, blacks earned only seventy Ph.D.'s in all the humanities.) Thus we must conclude that the growth of the field within the academy depends in part on increasing the number of minority students in our graduate programs. The keen competition among literature departments for talented job candidates is based on scarcity; it is incumbent on the members of the MLA to develop viable recruitment mechanisms that will continue to diversify our graduate student population.

What, finally, can we say about the concerns of Africanists and African-Americanists? Virtually no one, it seems clear, believes that the texts written by black authors cohere into a tradition because the authors share certain innate characteristics. Opposing the essentialism of European "universality" with a dark essentialism — an approach that in various ways had characterized a large component of black literary criticism since the black arts movement — has given way to subtler questions. What is following the critique of the essentialist notions that cloaked the text in a mantle of "blackness," replete with the accretions of all sorts of sociological clichés, is a "post-formal" resituation of texts, accounting for the social dynamism of subjection, incorporation, and marginalization in relation to the cultural dominant.

Black literature, recent critics seem to be saying, can no longer simply name the "margin." Close readings are increasingly naming the specificity of black texts, revealing the depth and range of cultural details far beyond the economic exploitation of blacks by whites. This increased focus on the specificity of the text has enabled us to begin to chart the patterns of repetition and revision among texts by black authors. In *Notes of a Native Son* James Baldwin described his own obsession with "race" in his fiction: "I have not written about being a Negro at such length because I expect that to be my only subject, but only because it was the gate I had to unlock before I could hope to write about anything else" (8). One must *learn* to be "black" in this society, precisely because "blackness" is a socially produced category. Accordingly, many black authors read and revise one another, address similar themes, and repeat the cultural and linguistic codes of a common symbolic geography. For these reasons, we can think of them as forming literary traditions.

We might think of the development of African-American criticism over the past two decades in four distinct stages, beginning with the black arts movement of the mid and late sixties. The black arts movement, whose leading theoreticians were Amiri Baraka and Larry Neal, was a reaction against the New Criticism's formalism. The readings these critics advanced were broadly cultural and richly contextualized; they aimed to be "holistic" and based formal literature firmly on black urban vernacular, expressive culture. Art was a fundamental part of "the people"; "art for art's sake" was seen to be a concept alien to a "pan-African" sensibility, a sensibility that was whole, organic, and, of course, quite ahistorical. What was identified as European or Western essentialism — masked under the rubric of "universality" — was attacked by asserting an oppositional black or "neo-African" essentialism. In place of formalist notions about art, these critics promoted a poetics rooted in a social realism, indeed, in a sort of mimeticism; the relation between black art and black life was a direct one.

In response to what we might think of as the social organicism of the black arts movement, a formalist organicism emerged in the mid-seventies. This movement was concerned with redirecting the critic's attention to the "literariness" of the black texts as autotelic artifacts, to their status as "acts of language" first and foremost. The use of formalist and structuralist theories and modes of reading characterized the criticism of this period. The formalists saw their work as a "corrective" to the social realism of the black arts critics.

In the third stage, critics of black literature began to retheorize social — and textual — boundaries. Drawing on poststructuralist theory as well as deriving theories from black expressive, vernacular culture, these critics were able to escape both the social organicism of the black arts movement and the formalist organicism of the "reconstructionists." Their work might be characterized as a "new black aesthetic" movement, though it problematizes the categories of both the "black" and the "aesthetic." An initial phase of theorizing has given way to the generation of close readings that attend to the "social text" as well. These critics use close readings to reveal cultural contradictions and the social aspects of literature, the larger dynamics of subjection and incorporation through which the subject is produced.

This aspect of contemporary African-American literary studies is related directly to recent changes in critical approaches to American studies generally. Black studies has functioned as a strategic site for autocritique within American studies itself. No longer, for example, are the concepts of "black" and "white" thought to be preconstituted; rather, they are mutually constitutive and socially produced. The theoretical work of feminist critics of African and African-American literature, moreover, has turned away from a naively additive notion of sexism and racism. Especially in this work, we have come to understand that critiques of "essentialism" are inadequate to explain the complex social dynamism of marginalized cultures.

Richard Wright once argued, polemically, that if white racism did not exist, then black literature would not exist, and he predicted the demise of the latter with the cessation of the former. It is difficult to deny that certain elements of African-American culture are the products of cross-cultural encounters with white racism. But black culture, these close readings reveal, is radically underdetermined by the social dynamism of white racism. While it is important to criticize nativistic essentialism, in doing so we can lose sight of the larger social dynamic, the things that make people come together into groups in the first place. Developments in African-American studies have helped to reveal the factitious nature of an "American" identity; that which had been systematically excluded has now been revoiced as a mainstream concern.

Works Cited

Applebee, Arthur N. *A Study of Book-Length Works Taught in High School English Courses.* Albany: Center for the Learning and Teaching of Literature, 1989.

Baldwin, James. "Here Be Dragons." *The Price of the Ticket: Collected Nonfiction, 1948–1985.* New York: St. Martin's, 1985. 677–90.

————. *Notes of a Native Son.* Boston: Beacon, 1955.

Benston, Kimberly. Letter to the author. 16 Sept. 1989.

Fiedler, Leslie, and Houston A. Baker, Jr., eds. *English Literature: Opening Up the Canon; Selected Papers from the*

English Institute, 1979. Baltimore: Johns Hopkins UP, 1981.

Fisher, Dexter, ed. *Minority Language and Literature: Retrospective and Perspective.* New York: MLA, 1977.

Fisher, Dexter, and Robert Stepto, eds. *Afro-American Literature: The Reconstruction of Instruction.* New York: MLA, 1979.

CHAPTER
6

Integrating the American Mind

When I'm asked to talk about the opening of the American mind, or the decentering of the humanities, or the new multiculturalism — or any number of such putative "developments" — I have to say my reaction is pretty much Mahatma Gandhi's when they asked him what he thought about Western civilization. He said he thought it would be a very good idea. My sentiments exactly.

This decade has, to be sure, witnessed an interesting coupling of trends. On the one hand, we've seen calls from on high to reclaim a legacy, to fend off the barbarians at the gates and return to some prelapsarian state of grace. On the other hand (or is it the same hand?), we've seen a disturbing recrudescence of campus racism sweeping the nation. Many of you will have seen the articles about this in the recent media, as the topic has been in the news for quite some time. For people who agitated in the civil rights era and saw real gains in the college curriculum in the 1970s, the new conservatism seems to have succeeded their own efforts rather as the Redemption politicians followed the Reconstruction, threatening to undo what progress had been made.

One thing is clear. Education in a democratic society (or in one that aspires to that ideal) has particular burdens placed upon it: few theorists of American education, in this century or the preceding one, have separated pedagogy from the needs of citizenship. The usual term, here, is often given a sinister intonation: *social reproduction*. Yet this country has always had an evolutionary view of what reproduction entails: we've never been content with more replication, we've sought improvement. We want our kids to be better than we are.

So it's discouraging, even painful, to look about our colleges, bastions of liberal education, and find that people are now beginning to talk—and with justice, it seems—about the "new racism." I don't want to offer a simple diagnosis, but perhaps the phenomenon isn't completely unconnected to larger political trends. It's been pointed out that today's freshmen were ten years old when the Reagan era began; presumably the public discourse of the 1980s had something to do with the forming of political sensibilities.

But whatever the causes, the climate on campus has been worsening: according to one monitoring group, racial incidents have been reported at over 175 colleges since the 1986–87 school year. And that's just counting the cases that made the papers.

At the same time, there's been, since 1977, a marked decline in overall black enrollment in colleges. The evidence suggests the decline is connected to a slipping economic situation, and to cuts in available federal aid. In the decade since 1977, federal grants and scholarships have fallen 62 percent, and that, of course, disproportionately affects minority students. Almost half of all black children (46.7 percent) live under the poverty line, according to the Congressional Research Service. Indeed, if you look at students at traditionally black colleges, you find that 42 percent of them come from families with income below the poverty line; a third of these students come from families with a total family income less than $6,000 a year. So when it comes to larger economic trends, blacks are like the canaries in the coal mine: the first to go when things are going wrong.

But there's an even bigger problem than getting these students, and that's keeping them. The attrition rate is depressing. At Berkeley, one in four black students will graduate. The fact is, according to the National Center of Education Statistics, that of freshmen blacks in 1980, only 31 percent had graduated by 1986. And while financial pressures explain some of it, they don't explain all of it.

Down the educational pike, things get worse. Just 4.0 percent of our full-time college professors are black, and the number is said to be decreasing. In 1986, only 820 of the 32,000 Ph.D.'s awarded went to blacks; less than half those 820 planned a college career (that's 0.015 percent of our new Ph.D.'s).

In short, it's a bad situation. But it's not a conspiracy; nobody wants it to be the way it is. In general, our colleges really are devoted to diversity: people are genuinely upset when they fail to incorporate diversity among their students and faculty. I said before that the peculiar charge of our education system is the shaping of a democratic polity. It's a reflection of the public consensus on this matter that one of the few bipartisan issues in the last presidential campaign had to do with equitable access to higher education. Pollsters on both sides found that this was an issue that made the American heart skip a beat. Equal opportunity in education is an idea with very broad appeal in this country. And that has something to do with what education means to us. So one thing I want to bring out is that the schools are a site where real contradictions and ambivalences are played out.

I would like to think about institutions for higher learning in terms of the larger objectives of what we call a liberal education; as unfashionable as it is among many of my fellow theorists, I do believe in the humanities, very broadly conceived. But it's that breadth of conception I want to address. We hear the complaints. Allan Bloom, for example, laments that "just at the moment when everyone else has become 'a person,' blacks have become blacks." (Needless to say, "everyone else" can become a person precisely when the category *person* comes to be defined in contradistinction to *black*.) Many thoughtful educators are dismayed, even bewildered, when minority students—at Berkeley or Stanford or Texas or Oberlin, the sentiment's widespread—say that they feel like visitors, like guests, like foreign or colonized citizens in relation to a traditional canon that fails to represent their cultural identities. I'm not interested in simply endorsing that sentiment; it's not a reasoned argument, this reaction, but it is a playing out—a logical extension— of an ideology resident in the traditional rhetoric about Western civilization. And I want to consider it in that light.

Once upon a time, there was a race of men who could claim all of knowledge as their purview. Someone like Francis Bacon really did try to organize all of knowledge into a single capacious but coherent structure. And even into the nineteenth century, the creed of universal knowledge—*mathesis universalis*—still reigned. There's a wonderful piece of nineteenth-century student doggerel about Jowett, the Victorian classicist and master of Balliol College, Oxford, which rather sums up the philosophy:

Here stand I, my name is Jowett,
If there's knowledge, then I know it;
I am the master of this college,
What I know not, is not knowledge.

The question this raises for us, of course, is: How does something get to count as knowledge? Intellectuals, Gramsci famously observes, can be defined as experts in legitimation. And the academy, today, is an institution of legitimation—establishing what counts as knowledge, what counts as culture. In the most spirited attacks on the movement toward multiculturalism in the academy today, there's a whiff of this: We are the masters of this college—What we know not, is not knowledge. So that in the wake of Bacon's epistemic megalomania, there's been a contrary movement, a constriction of what counts as even worth knowing. We've got our culture, what more do we need? Besides, there was Heidegger on stage right, assuring us that "philosophy speaks Greek." And beyond the cartography of Western culture? A cryptic warning: Here Be Monsters.

I got mine: The rhetoric of liberal education remains suffused with the imagery of possession, patrimony, legacy, lineage, inheritance—call it cultural geneticism (in the broadest sense of that term). At the same moment, the rhetoric of possession and lineage subsists upon, and perpetuates, a division: between us and them, we the heirs of *our* tradition, and you, the Others, whose difference defines our identity. (In the French colonies, in Africa and the Caribbean, a classroom of African students would dutifully read from their textbook, "Our ancestors, the Gauls . . . " Well, you could see that wasn't going to last.)

What happens, though, if you buy into that rhetoric—if you accept its terms and presuppositions about cultural geneticism? Then you will say: Yes, I am Other, and if the aim of education is to reinforce an individual's rightful cultural legacy, then I don't belong here—I am a guest at someone else's banquet. Foucault called this kind of contestation that of "reverse discourse": it remains entrapped within the presuppositions of the discourse it means to oppose, enacts a conflict internal to that "master discourse"; but when the terms of argument have already been defined, it may look like the only form of contestation possible.

One of the most eloquent reflections on this sense of entrapment is James Baldwin's, where the rhetoric of dispossession turns to that of cultural reappropriation:

> I know, in any case, that the most crucial time in my own development came when I was forced to recognize that I was a kind of bastard of the West; when I followed the line of my past I did not find myself in Europe but in Africa. And this meant that in some subtle way, in a really profound way, I brought to Shakespeare, Bach, Rembrandt, to the stones of Paris, to the cathedral at Chartres, and to the Empire State Building, *a special attitude.* These were not really my reactions, they did not contain my history; I might search in them in vain forever for any reflection of myself. I was an interloper; this was not my heritage. At the same time, I had no other heritage which I could possibly hope to use—I had certainly been unfitted for the jungle or the tribe. I would have to appropriate these white centuries, I would have to make them mine—I would have to accept my special attitude, my special place in this scheme—otherwise I would have no place in any scheme.

(This terror of having no place in any scheme contrasts oddly with the more familiar modernist anxiety of the Western writer, the anxiety that one fits into a scheme all too easily, all too well.)

If Richard Wright's comments are characteristically blunter, they are no less anxious: "I'm black. I'm a man of the West. . . . I see and understand the non- or anti-Western point of view." But, Wright confesses, "when I look out upon the vast stretches of this earth inhabited by brown, black and yellow men . . . my reactions and attitudes are those of the West" (*White Man, Listen!*). Wright never had clearer insight into himself; but his ambivalent relation to both the Western and non-Western cultures was satisfactorily resolved. So long as we retain a vocabulary of heritage and inheritance in defining our putative national cultures, it cannot *be* resolved.

This suggests (if I may invoke the relevant stereotypes) that the old fogey and the Young Turk have a lot more in common then they realize; that they may, in fact, be two sides of the same debased coin; and that those of us who really care about humane learning should convert to another currency.

The argument has been made that cultural nationalism has been a constitutive aspect of Western education. As humanists, our challenge today is, simply, to learn to live without it. Indeed, it saddens me that there should be any perceived conflict between the ideal of humanistic learning and what I think of as the truly human, and humane, version of the humanities, one that sees the West not as some mythical, integrative whole, but as a part of a still larger whole. In the resonant words of W.E.B. Du Bois:

> I sit with Shakespeare, and he winces not. Across the color line I move arm in arm with Balzac and Dumas, where smiling men and welcoming women glide in gilded halls. From out the caves of evening that swing between the strong-limbed earth and the tracery of the stars, I summon Aristotle and Aurelius and what soul I will, and they come all graciously with no scorn nor condescension. So, wed with Truth, I dwell above the Veil. Is this the life you grudge us, O knightly America? Is this the life you long to change into

the dull red hideousness of Georgia? Are you so afraid lest peering from this high Pisgah, between Philistine and Amalekite, we sight the Promised Land?

Which is then to say, I believe we can change the terms of argument; I believe we can rethink the role of a liberal education without the conceptual residue of cultural nationalism or geneticism. I believe it, because I do think many scholars have already begun to do so.

And some people have begun to realize that broadening our educational vistas is not only sweet, but useful. As most of you will know, a panel of U.S. governors recently concluded that America's economic and cultural dominance has been endangered by our vast ignorance of the languages and cultures of other nations. In a report made public recently, the National Governors Association argued for broad changes in the way we teach foreign languages and basic geography.

Among the report's more startling findings are the following:

- A recent Gallup poll revealed that young American adults know less about geography than their peers in six developed countries.
- One in seven American adults cannot locate the United States on a world map.
- Twenty-five percent of a sample of high school seniors in Dallas did not know that Mexico was the country bordering the United States to the south.
- Only 20 percent of American high school graduates receive more than two years' instruction in a foreign language.

In response to this report, Ernest L. Boyer, the president of the Carnegie Foundation for the Advancement of Teaching, remarked that "a curriculum with international perspective" is "critically important to the future of our nation."

Well, Americans know so very little about world history and culture in part because high school and college core curricula, in this country, center upon European and American societies, with America represented as the logical conclusion or summary of civilization since the Greeks, in the same way that Christians believe that Christ is the culmination of the Old Testament prophesies. Our ignorance of physical geography is a symptom of a much broader ignorance of the world's cultural geography. Since the trivium and quadrivium of the Latin Middle Ages, "the humanities" has *not* meant the best that has been thought by all human beings; rather, "the humanities" has meant the best that has been thought by white males in the Greco-Roman, Judeo-Christian traditions. A tyrannical pun obtains between the words *humanity,* on the one hand, and *humanities,* on the other.

We need to reform our entire notion of core curricula to account for the comparable eloquence of the African, the Asian, the Latin American, and the Middle Eastern traditions, to prepare our students for their roles in the twenty-first century as citizens of a world culture, educated through a truly human notion of the humanities.

Now, I talked earlier about the long-dead ideal of universal knowledge. Today, you look back to C. P. Snow's complaint about the gulf between the "two cultures," and you think, *two?* Keep counting, C. P. The familiar buzz words here are the "fragmentation of humanistic knowledge." And there are people who think that the decentering of the humanities that I advocate just makes a bad situation worse: Bring on the Ivory Towers of Babel. So I want to say a few words about this.

There are, certainly, different kinds of fragmentation. One kind of fragmentation is just the inevitable result of the knowledge explosion; specialized fields produce specialized knowledge, and there's too much to keep up with. But there's another kind of fragmentation which does deserve scrutiny: the ways in which knowledge produced in one discipline setting is inaccessible to scholars in another discipline, even when it would be useful to them in solving their problems. And here, what I call the decentering of the humanities can help us rethink some of the ways traditional subjects are constituted and can allow us a critical purchase helpful in cultural studies quite generally. Indeed, far from being inimical to traditional Western scholarship, humanistic scholarship in Asian and African cultures can be mutually enriching to it, to the humanities in general.

And that's as you'd expect: The study of the humanities is the study of the possibilities of human life in culture. It thrives on diversity. And when you get down to cases, it's hard to deny that what you could call the new scholarship has invigorated the traditional disciplines. Historians of black America, for example, have pioneered work in oral history that's had a significant effect on the way nineteenth-century social history is done. A much older example: Think of the upheavals in Homeric scholarship from Milman Parry's work on those Yugoslavian bards, or of the advances in understanding the epic from Jack Goody's studies of northern Ghanaian orature. In art history, many Africanists have helped introduce ways of approaching artwork that takes a rich and sophisticated account of cultural context.

Often it's when unfamiliar cultural formations are explored that the inadequacies of traditional disciplinary boundaries in the Western academy are mostly clearly shown up. The gap between the social sciences and the humanities is often bemoaned by those studying the complexities of African history and cultural forms. As Kwame Appiah observes, "methods normally used in anthropology and in art-history, for example, can provide profound and mutually reinforcing illumination of the cultural significance of a masquerade or the architecture of a shrine, but students and scholars who are taught to see these methods as radically incommensurable are bound to fail to achieve these insights." Appiah continues:

> Those scholars who have faced up to these challenges have had to develop theoretical and methodological tools and data resources that promise help in thinking creatively about the ways in which society and culture relate to each other quite generally. In short, the challenges posed by [for example] African materials and the new approaches and techniques developed to deal with the varieties of African experience, offer an opportunity to enrich and expand the perspectives of all humanities disciplines and to aid in casting off disciplinary blinders.

In literary theory, our understanding of expressive acts and the symbolic have been influenced by, for instance, Victor Turner's work on the Ndembu; and if you're reading a new historicist essay on drama in Renaissance England, don't be surprised to encounter references to Clifford Geertz's work on the Balinese. I don't want to exaggerate the gains: the opening up of traditional disciplines to the scholarly insights of the new has only just begun and hasn't progressed as far as it might have.

But I do want to emphasize that a true decentering of the humanities can't be just a matter of new content in old forms. We have to get away from the paradigm of disciplinary essentialism: imagining the boundaries of disciplines as hermetic, imagining our architectures of knowledge as natural or organic. Granted, sometimes conversation is neither possible nor productive. But we don't need a lazy sort of Platonism that can pretend to "cut nature at the joints" — sustaining the illusion only as long as we don't inquire too closely about the peculiar institutional history of our own particular discipline.

I've suggested that moving toward this human notion of the humanities moves us away from the divisive us/them implications of traditional defenses of the humanities and removes a source of cultural alienation that is clearly breeding disenchantment and disillusionment among those to whom the experience of higher education may matter the most. But I also think—and here my Whiggish triumphalism is revealed—that it's the natural conclusion of scholarly enlightenment, in which ethnocentric presuppositions have fallen under scholarly critique—autocritique—and been found wanting. We need, for instance, to rethink the whole notion of comparative literature. The most influential and innovative programs in comparative literature have usually embraced just three languages—Latin, French, German—and one other. I look forward to truly comparative programs of comparative literature that embrace the languages and literatures of Yoruba, Urdu, or Arabic as well as the traditional European literatures. I think we should design a required Humanities Course that's truly humanistic—with the Western segment comprising a quarter or a third—in addition to the traditional Western Civ course, so that students can begin to understand the histories of civilization itself, in a truly comparative manner. Such an embracive posture honors the best, the noblest traditions and ambitions of the academy. And while I've decried cultural nationalism, I hope you'll permit me to bow to it in citing something Ishmael Reed has said on the subject of multiculturalism. He said it's possible here "because the United States is unique in the world: *the world is here.*"

Or listen to a great canonical author, Herman Melville, writing a century earlier: "There is something in the contemplation of the mode in which America has been settled, that, in a noble breast, should forever extinguish the prejudices of national dislikes. Settled by the people of all nations, all nations may claim her for their own. You can not spill a drop of American blood, without spilling the blood of the whole world. . . . We are not a narrow tribe, no: our blood is as the flood of the Amazon, made up of a thousand noble currents, all pouring into one. We are not a nation, so much as a world."

In a more practical vein: It turns out that the affirmative action programs for recruiting minority faculty have been successful only at institutions where strong ethnic studies programs exist. Many ambitious "minority" scholars of my generation, feeling secure in their academic credentials and their ethnic identities, have tried to fill a lacuna they perceived in their own education by producing scholarship about, well, "their own people." A lot of the social commitment that emerged during the 1960s has been redirected to the scholarly arena: continents of ignorance have been explored and charted. At the same time, "minority studies" (so-called) are not "for" minorities, any more than "majority studies" (let's say) are for majorities. And it is wrong simply to conflate affirmative action objectives in employment with the teaching of such subjects.

I respect what Robert Nisbet calls the Academic Dogma: knowledge for its own sake (I suspect it doesn't quite exist; but that's another matter). At the same time, I believe that truly humane learning can't help but expand the constricted boundaries of human sympathy, of social tolerance. Maybe the truest thing to be said about racism is that it represents a profound failure of imagination. I've talked a good deal about cultural pluralism as a good in itself, as the natural shape of scholarship untrammeled by narrow ethnocentrism. And the best ethnic studies departments have made a real contribution to this ideal of scholarly diversity. As I said, I respect the ideal of the disinterested pursuit of knowledge, however unattainable, and I don't think classes should be converted into consciousness-raising sessions, Lord knows; at the same time, anyone who's not a positivist realizes that "moral education" is a pleonasm: in the humanities, facts and values don't exist in neatly disjunct regimes of knowledge. Allan Bloom is right to ask about the effect of higher education on our kids' moral development, even though that's probably the only thing he is right about.

Amy Gutmann said something important in her recent book *Democratic Education:* "In a democracy, political disagreement is not something that we should generally seek to avoid. Political controversies over our educational problems are a particularly important source of social progress because they have the potential for educating so many citizens." I think that's true; I think a lot of us feel that any clamor or conflict over the curriculum is just a bad thing in itself, that it somehow undermines the legitimacy of the institutions of knowledge — a sort of no-news-is-good-news attitude on the subject of education; they think if you even look at a university cross-eyed, it'll dry up and blow away and then where will you be? In contrast, I think one of the most renewing activities we can do is to rethink the institutions where we teach people to think; we invest in myths of continuity, but universities have constantly been molting and creating themselves anew for the last millennium, and there's no reason to think that'll change in the next. Gerald Graff has been saying, where there's no consensus — and there's no consensus — teach the conflicts. In fact, I think at the better colleges, we do. We don't seem to be able not to. And that's nothing to be embarrassed about: College isn't kindergarten, and our job isn't to present a seemly, dignified, unified front to the students. College students are too old to *form* — we shouldn't delude ourselves — but they're not too old to challenge. I'm reminded of something that the college president and educator Robert Maynard Hutchins wrote, in a book he published during the height of the McCarthy era. He recounted a conversation he'd had with a distinguished doctor about the attempt of the Board of Regents of the University of California to extort (as Hutchins put it) "an illegal and unconstitutional oath of loyalty from the faculty of that great institution." "Yes, but" the doctor said, "if we are going to hire these people to look after our children we are entitled to know what their opinions are." And Hutchins grandly remarked, "I think it is clear that the collapse of liberal education in the United States is related as cause or effect or both to the notion that professors are people who are hired to look after children." Wise words, those.

In all events, the sort of pluralism I've been recommending has one evolutionary advantage over its opponents. If you ask, How do we form a consensus around such a "de-centering" proposal? the answer is that it doesn't exactly require a consensus. Which is why, in the words of John Dewey, "pluralism is the greatest philosophical idea of our times." Not that this puts us home free. As Dewey also said,

> What philosophers have got to do is to work out a fresh analysis of the relations between the one and the many. Our shrinking world presents that issue today in a thousand different forms. . . . How are we going to make the most of the new values we set on variety, difference, and individuality — how are we going to realize their possibilities in every field, and at the same time not sacrifice that plurality to the cooperation we need so much? How can we bring things together as we must without losing sight of plurality?

Learning without center is not learning without focus. We've all seen undigested eclecticism posing as a bold new synthesis; but to read and write culture anew means additional demands for rigor and coherence, not emancipation from these things. I take Dewey's question seriously, but there's nothing vaporous about the form the answer takes: it is made of brick and mortar, and sometimes a little ivy about the architrave. For us — scholars and teachers — it is the university, whose constant refashioning is our charge, burden, and privilege.

CHAPTER
7

African-American Studies in the 21st Century

For a woman or a person of color, there has never been a more exciting and rewarding time to be in the academy than today. More women and black people are tenured than ever before, and more occupy tenure-track positions.

We are in the midst of a renaissance of black scholarship, both individual and collective. Robin Williams and Gerald Jaynes' *A Common Destiny*, an updated study of the social and economic status of the black American since the Myrdal Report; Darlene Clarke Hines's monumental attempt to make systematic the scholarly literature about the social status and intellectual history of black women in the nineteenth and twentieth centuries; Charles V. Hamilton's encompassing *Encyclopedia of Black Culture*, now under way at Columbia; the Schomburg Library of 19th Century Black Women's Writings, published in forty volumes; the *Oxford Companion to African American Literature* and the *Norton Anthology of African American Literature*, both to be published within the next few years; the Black Papers Projects, including the collected works of Frederick Douglass, Zora Neale Hurston, Booker T. Washington, Marcus Garvey, the black abolitionists, and the papers of the Freedman's Bureau; the Black Periodical Literature Project — these are merely some of the research projects that are well under way and in need of the support of foundations.

The particular burden of scholars of Afro-American studies is that we must often resurrect the texts of our tradition before we can even begin to analyze them. Few foundations have begun to acknowledge the importance of supporting this kind of "foundational" research — the sort of project that consolidates previous gains in research in the field; the sort of project that enables the work of other, younger scholars, of generations to come; the sort of work that provides a starting place for those who will come after us. I am speaking here of bibliographies, concordances, dictionaries, and encyclopedias. (My own great dream is to edit the Encyclopedia Africana, a project first defined by W.E.B. Du Bois in 1910, and to edit which he emigrated to Ghana in 1961 at Kwame Nkrumah's request.) This sort of research may be unglamorous, but it is indispensable.

For black culture in America is a national concern, a region in the broadest sense of that term — a region of the collective and richly diverse cultural mind of America. As we face the twenty-first century, changing demographics within our population — in which a majority of our citizens will be people of color by the year 2020 — have impelled people to rethink the shape and function of our national cultural institutions, and indeed of the way that we define the relation between being "human" and what we think of as the "humanities" and the "arts." For America has always been a multicultural state.

Equal access to the arts and the humanities, broadly reconceived, is the most important cultural project upon which we can embark in this last decade of the twentieth century, as we seek to prepare our students and thereby our society to be meaningful parts of a twenty-first-century world culture. For the humanities and the arts are the common property of us all.

Our generation must record, codify, and disseminate the assembled data about African and African-American culture, thereby institutionalizing the received knowledge about African-Americans that has been gathered for the past century, and that we continue to gather, as we chart heretofore unexplored continents of ignorance. For our generation of scholars in African-American studies, to map the splendid diversity of human life in culture is the charge of the scholar of African-American Studies.

Each of us in African-American studies entered the field in part, I believe, to undertake scholarly research that would fill those lacunae that we encountered in our own undergraduate educations, and to make a political statement—whether an explicit political statement or an implicit political statement—about the intellect and the intellectual attainments of persons of African descent in the Old and New Worlds. Many of us were tutored by the true greats of the field—St. Clair Drake, Margaret Walker, Rayford Logan, Darwin Turner, Saunders Redding, Charles Davis, Kenneth Dike, and Sterling Brown, to name only a few—many of whom are now sadly dead. We are the generation of leaders in African-American studies, and it is with our generation of scholars that our field, our discipline, shall rise or fall.

How do we do this? How do we ensure the permanent institutionalization of our field, within the larger American academy? How do we address, if not resolve, that certain tension between the facts that, on one hand, there has never been a better time to be a person of color and a member of the academy, and that, on the other hand, there has scarcely been a worse time to be black in

America, that we are doing vastly better in the academy and the curriculum than we are in the streets, even though both the multicultural movement and African-American studies are under a surprisingly sustained attack from the cultural right?

I believe that an agenda for the twenty-first century must include an emphasis upon cultural studies and public policy, as two broad and fruitful rubrics under which to organize our discipline. Under cultural studies, we must continue to develop the strongest critical impulse to explicate our culture's achievements in literature, music, film, religion, the visual arts, the dance, and the other forms of expressive culture, developing strong institutional links between our universities and our local and national cultural organizations, in order to facilitate their growth and permanence.

In public policy matters, our involvement is crucial and urgent. For outside of the academy — and this irony is a painful one — there has rarely been a worse time to be young and black. One black man is in prison for every two black men in college; homicide is the leading cause of death for young black men, and three of every four black women, it is estimated, will be pregnant by the age of twenty. Add to this the functional illiteracy rate and the unemployment rate, and we realize that the "two nations" predicted by the Kerner Commission Report in 1968 may very well be upon us. And yet, if the Iraq war taught us anything, it is that this country can mobilize billions of dollars virtually overnight whenever it wants to. Let us collectively call for a Marshall Plan for our cities. Let us use the National Academy of Sciences $2-million study, *A Common Destiny,* and — in concert with the Joint Center, our civil rights organizations, civic groups, the black church, and the Congressional Black Caucus — take steps to counter and reverse the governmental neglect of America's cities that began in the late

1970s. Is it beyond us to create the kinds of job-training programs that can convert the permanently unemployed to the eminently employable? Federal scholarship assistance, as has been demonstrated a hundred times, *raises* the number of blacks who matriculate. College education should not be a luxury reserved for the affluent few. Our public schools should be centers of nurture and instruction, not laboratories for drugs and crime. And we know that none of these problems has to be intractable. James Comer's major experiments in the New Haven school system — recently acknowledged with a $15-million grant from the Rockefeller Foundation — demonstrate the headway that commitment and common sense can make. Public school curricula, from prekindergarten through grade 12, should enable our young people to learn systematically — but not only — about the forces that have shaped their cultural identities. African-American Studies scholars should, properly, be at the heart of all of these endeavors, and not peripheral to them. These things, after all, are what our field is about and has been about since its formal inception some two decades ago.

Within the academy, I believe, we must seek to explore the hyphen in African-American, on both sides of the Atlantic, by charting the porous relations between African-American culture and an "American" culture that officially, even today, pretends that an Anglo-American *regional* culture is the true, universal culture, and that African-American culture is, at best, a subset of it or a substandard and subservient deviant of it.

We must chart both the moments of continuity and discontinuity between African cultures and African-American cultures. Only a fool would try to deny continuities between the Old World and the New World African cultures. But equally misguided, needless to say, is any attempt to chart those continuities on the basis of a mystified and dubious biological or so-called racial science. Above all else, we are a people who were constructed as members of a new Pan-African ethnicity. We cannot — and should not — deny the historical contingencies of this construction, lay claim to the ideal of "blackness" as an ideology or a quasi religion, totalized and essentialized into a protofascist battering ram supervised by official thought police.

I remember when I was a student at Cambridge, I was about to have my first supervision with Wole Soyinka, then in exile from Nigeria, on African literature. And though I was only twenty-two, I was certain I had a deep understanding of African culture. I had read Jahnheinz Jahn's *Muntu,* you see, and was fired up with the inspirational *doxa* of *nommo,* which was the master concept, the distilled essence, of all African culture. "I hope you know something about Africa," Soyinka told me as I came for my supervision, viewing my Afro balefully. "Absolutely," I said, having just memorized the principles of *nommo* in preparation for our meeting. "Because the fact is," Soyinka added, "the only reason I accepted you as a student was that at least you didn't talk about that *nommo* nonsense." "*Nommo?*" I said. "Never heard of it."

Those were, of course, the days when such facile and reductive concepts promulgated by good-hearted and systematic authors, often from Europe, threatened to eclipse the real specificities of Africa's richly diverse cultural life. Soyinka's wariness was certainly justified. As satisfying as these one-size-fits-all, all-in-one rubrics were, they made real cultural work well-nigh impossible. So, too, with the romantic racisms of an earlier era. As the Benin philosopher Adotevi once remarked, "Negritude is the *black* way of being white."

We are scholars. For our field to grow, we need to encourage a true proliferation of ideologies and methodologies, rather than to seek uniformity or conformity. An ideal department of African-American Studies would have several of these approaches represented, rather than merely one officially sanctioned approach to a very complex subject. African-American Studies should be the home of free inquiry into the very complexity of being of African descent in the world, rather than a place where we seek to essentialize our cultural selves into stasis, and to drown out critical inquiry.

And while I for one wish that all persons of color would pursue our discipline on one level or another during their undergraduate careers, our subject is open to all — whether to study or to teach. After all, the fundamental premise of the academy is that all things ultimately are knowable; all are therefore teachable. What would we say to a person who said that we couldn't teach Milton because we are not Anglo-Saxon, or male, or heterosexual — or blind! We do nothing to help our discipline by attempting to make of it the equivalent of a closed shop, where only blacks need apply. On the other hand, to say that ethnic identity is socially constructed is not to say that it is somehow unreal, to deny the complexities of our own positionality, to claim that these are not differences that make a difference.

We cannot, finally, succumb to the temptation to resurrect our own version of the Thought Police, who would determine who, and what, is "black." "Mirror, Mirror on the Wall, Who's the Blackest One of All?" is a question best left behind in the sixties. If we allow ourselves to succumb to the urge to build an academic discipline around this perverse question, we will, like the fairy-tale witch, die from our own poison. For if the coming century in this country is multicolored, it is a blackness without blood that *we* must pass on.

III

SOCIETY

8

"What's in a Name?" Some Meanings of Blackness

The question of color takes up much space in these pages, but the question of color, especially in this country, operates to hide the graver questions of the self.

—JAMES BALDWIN, 1961

. . . blood, darky, Tar Baby, Kaffir, shine . . . moor, blackamoor, Jim Crow, spook . . . quadroon, meriney, red bone, high yellow . . . Mammy, porch monkey, home, homeboy, George . . . spear-chucker, schwarze, Leroy, Smokey . . . mouli, buck, Ethiopian, brother, sistah. . . .

—TREY ELLIS, 1989

I had forgotten the incident completely, until I read Trey Ellis's essay, "Remember My Name," in a recent issue of the *Village Voice* (June 13, 1989). But there, in the middle of an extended italicized list of the bynames of "the race" ("the race" or "our people" being the terms my parents used in polite or reverential discourse, "jigaboo" or "nigger" more commonly used in anger, jest, or pure disgust) it was: "George." Now the events of that very brief exchange return to mind so vividly that I wonder why I had forgotten it.

My father and I were walking home at dusk from his second job. He "moonlighted" as a janitor in the evenings for the telephone company. Every day but Saturday, he would come home at 3:30 from his regular job at the paper mill, wash up, eat supper, then at 4:30 head downtown to his second job. He used to make jokes frequently about a union official who moonlighted. I never got the joke, but he and his friends thought it was hilarious. All I knew was that my family always ate well, that my brother and I had new clothes to wear, and that all of the white people in Piedmont, West Virginia, treated my parents with an odd mixture of resentment and respect that even we understood at the time had something directly to do with a small but certain measure of financial security.

He had left a little early that evening because I was with him and I had to be in bed early. I could not have been more than five or six, and we had stopped off at the Cut-Rate Drug Store (where no black person in town but my father could sit down to eat, and eat off real plates with real silverware) so that I could buy some caramel ice cream, two scoops in a wafer cone, please, which I was busy licking when Mr. Wilson walked by.

Mr. Wilson was a very quiet white man, whose stony, brooding, silent manner seemed designed to scare off any overtures of friendship, even from white people. He was Irish, as was one third of our village (another third being Italian), the more affluent among whom sent their children to "Catholic School" across the bridge in Maryland. He had white straight hair, like my Uncle Joe, whom he uncannily resembled, and he carried a black worn metal lunch pail, the kind that Riley carried on the television show. My father always spoke to him, and for reasons that we never did understand, he always spoke to my father.

"Hello, Mr. Wilson," I heard my father say.

"Hello, George."

I stopped licking my ice cream cone and asked my Dad in a loud voice why Mr. Wilson had called him "George."

"Doesn't he know your name, Daddy? Why don't you tell him your name? Your name isn't George."

For a moment I tried to think of who Mr. Wilson was mixing Pop up with. But we didn't have any Georges among the colored people in Piedmont; nor were there colored Georges living in the neighboring towns and working at the mill.

"Tell him your name, Daddy."

"He knows my name, boy," my father said after a long pause. "He calls all colored people George."

A long silence ensued. It was "one of those things," as my mom would put it. Even then, that early, I knew when I was in the presence of "one of those things," one of those things that provided a glimpse, through a rent curtain, at another world that we could not affect but that affected us. There would be a painful moment of silence, and you would wait for it to give way to a discussion of a black superstar such as Sugar Ray or Jackie Robinson.

"Nobody hits better in a clutch than Jackie Robinson."

"That's right. Nobody."

I never again looked Mr. Wilson in the eye.

■　■　■

But I loved the names that we gave ourselves when no white people were around. And I have to confess that I have never really cared too much about what we called ourselves publicly, except when my generation was fighting the elders for the legitimacy of the word *black* as our common, public name. "I'd rather they called me 'nigger,'" my Uncle Raymond would say again and again. "I can't *stand* the way they say the word *black*. And, by the way," he would conclude, his dark brown eyes flashing as he looked with utter disgust at my tentative Afro, "when are you going to get that nappy shit *cut?*"

There was enough in our public name to make a whole generation of Negroes rail against our efforts to legitimize, to naturalize, the word *black*. Once we were black, I thought, we would be free, inside at least, and maybe from inside we would project a freedom outside of ourselves. "Free your mind," the slogan went, "and your behind will follow." Still, I value those all-too-rare, precious moments when someone "slips," in the warmth and comfort of intimacy, and says the dreaded words: "Was he colored?"

I knew that there was power in our name, enough power so that the prospect frightened my maternal uncles. To open the "Personal Statement" for my Yale admission application in 1968, I had settled upon the following: "My grandfather was colored, my father is Negro, and I am black." (If that doesn't grab them, I thought, then nothing will.) I wonder if my daughters, nine years hence, will adapt the line, identifying themselves as "I am an African-American." Perhaps they'll be Africans by then, or even feisty rapper-dappers. Perhaps, by that time, the most radical act of naming will be a return to "colored."

I began to learn about the meanings of blackness — or at least how to give voice to what I had experienced — when I went off to Yale. The class of 1973 was the first at Yale to include a "large" contingent of "Afro-Americans," the name we quickly and comfortably seized upon at New Haven. Like many of us in those years, I gravitated to courses in Afro-American studies, at least one per semester, despite the fact that I was pre-med, like almost all the other black kids at Yale—that is, until the ranks were devastated by organic chemistry. (Pre-law was the most common substitute.) The college campus, then, was a refuge from explicit racism, freeing us to read and write about our "racial" selves, to organize for recruitment of minority students and faculty, and to demand the constitutional rights of the Black Panther Party for Self-Defense—an action that led, at New Haven at least, to a full-fledged strike in April of 1970, two weeks before Nixon and Kissinger invaded Cambodia. The campus was our sanctuary, where we could be as black as the ace of spades and nobody seemed to mind.

Today the white college campus is a rather different place. Black studies, where it has survived—and it has survived only at those campuses where *someone* believed enough in its academic integrity to insist upon a sound academic foundation—is entering its third decade. More black faculty members are tenured than ever before, despite the fact that only eight hundred or so Afro-Americans took the doctorate in 1989, and fully half of these were in education. Yet for all the gains that have been made, racial tensions on college campuses appear to be on the rise. The dream of the university as a haven of racial equity, as an ultimate realm beyond the veil, has not been realized. Racism on our college campuses has become a palpable, ugly thing.

Even I—despite a highly visible presence as a faculty member at Cornell—have found it necessary to cross the street, hum a tune, or smile when confronting a lone white woman in a campus building or on the Commons late at night. (Once a white coed even felt it necessary to spring from an elevator that I was about to enter, in the very building where my department is housed.) Nor can

I help but feel some humiliation as I try to put a white person at ease in a dark place on campus at night, coming from nowhere, confronting that certain look of panic in his or her eyes, trying to think grand thoughts like Du Bois but—for the life of me—looking to him or her like Wille Horton. Grinning, singing, scratching my head, I have felt like Steppin Fetchit with a Ph.D. So much for Yale; so much for Cambridge.

■ ■ ■

The meanings of blackness are vastly more complex, I suspect, than they ever have been before in our American past. But how to explain? I have often imagined encountering the ghost of the great Du Bois, riding on the shoulders of the Spirit of Blackness.

"Young man," he'd say, "what has happened in my absence? Have things changed?"

"Well, sir," I'd respond, "your alma mater, Fair Harvard, has a black studies department, a Du Bois Research Center, and even a Du Bois Professor of History. Your old friend Thurgood Marshall sits like a minotaur as an associate justice on the Supreme Court. Martin Luther King's birthday is a *federal* holiday, and a black man you did not know won several Democratic presidential primaries last year. Black women novelists adorn the *New York Times* best-seller lists, and the number one television show in the country is a situation comedy concerning the lives and times of a refined Afro-American obstetrician and his lovely wife, who is a senior partner in a Wall Street law firm. Sammy Davis, Jr.'s second autobiography has been widely—"

"Young man, I have come a long way. Do not trifle with the Weary Traveler."

"I would not think of it, sir. I revere you, sir, why, I even—"

"How many of them had to die? How many of our

own? Did Nkrumah and Azikwe send troops? Did a nuclear holocaust bring them to their senses? When Shirley
Graham and I set sail for Ghana, I pronounced all hope
for our patient people doomed."

"No, sir," I would respond. "The gates of segregation
fell rather quickly after 1965. A new middle class defined
itself, a talented tenth, the cultured few, who, somehow,
slipped through the cracks."

"Then the preservation of the material base proved to
be more important then the primal xenophobia that we
had posited?"

"That's about it, Doctor. But regular Negroes still
catch hell. In fact, the ranks of the black underclass have
never been larger."

I imagine the great man would heave a sigh, as the
Spirit of Blackness galloped away.

From 1831, if not before, to 1965, an ideology of desegregation, of "civil rights," prevailed among our thinkers. Abolitionists, Reconstructors, neoabolitionists, all
shared one common belief: If we could only use the legis-
lature and the judiciary to create and interpret the laws
of desegregation and access, all else would follow. As it
turns out, it was vastly easier to dismantle the petty forms
of apartheid in this country (housing, marriage, hotels,
and restaurants) than anyone could have possibly believed it would be, *without* affecting the larger patterns
of inequality. In fact, the economic structure has not
changed one jot, in any fundamental sense, except that
black adult and teenage unemployment are much higher
now than they have been in my lifetime. Considering the
out-of-wedlock birthrate, the high school dropout rate,
and the unemployment figures, the "two nations" predicted by the Kerner Commission in 1968 may be upon
us. And the conscious manipulation of our public image,
by writers, filmmakers, and artists, which many of us

still seem to think will bring freedom, has had very little impact in palliating our structural social problems. What's the most popular television program in South Africa? The "Cosby Show." Why not?

■ ■ ■

Ideology, paradoxically, was impoverished when we needed it most, during the civil rights movement of the early 1960s. Unable to theorize what Cornel West calls "the racial problematic," unwilling (with very few exceptions) to theorize class, and scarcely able even to contemplate the theorizing of the curious compound effect of class-cum-race, we have—since the day after the signing of the Civil Rights Act of 1965—utterly lacked any instrumentality of ideological analysis, beyond the attempts of the Black Power and Black Aesthetic movements, to *invert* the signification of "blackness" itself. Recognizing that what had passed for "the human," or "the universal" was in fact white essentialism, we substituted one sort of essentialism (that of "blackness") for another. That, we learned quickly enough, was just not enough. But it led the way to a gestural politics captivated by fetishes and feel-bad rhetoric. The ultimate sign of our sheer powerlessness is all of the attention that we have given, in the past few months, to declaring the birth of the African-American and pronouncing the Black Self dead. Don't we have anything better to do?

Now, I myself happen to like African-American, especially because I am, as a scholar, an Africanist as well as an African-Americanist. Certainly the cultural continuities among African, Caribbean, and black American cultures cannot be denied. (The irony is that we often thought of ourselves as "African" until late into the nineteenth century. The death of the African was declared by the Park school of sociology in the first quarter of this century, which thought that the hyphenated ethnicity of the Negro American would prove to be ultimately liberating.) But so tame and unthreatening is a politics centered on onomastics that even the *New York Times*, in a major editorial, declared its support of this movement:

> If Mr. Jackson is right and blacks now prefer to be called African-Americans, it is a sign not just of their maturity but of the nation's success. . . . Blacks may now feel comfortable enough in their standing as citizens to adopt the family surname: American. And their first name, African, conveys a pride in cultural heritage that all Americans cherish. The late James Baldwin once lamented, "Nobody knows my name." Now everyone does. (December 22, 1988)

To which one young black writer, Trey Ellis, responded recently: "When somebody tries to tell me what to call myself in all uses just because they come to some decision at a cocktail party to which I wasn't even invited, my mama raised me to tell them to kiss my ass" (*Village Voice*, June 13, 1989). As he says, sometimes African-American just won't do.

■ ■ ■

Ellis's amused rejoinder speaks of a very different set of concerns and made me think of James Baldwin's prediction of the coming of a new generation that would give voice to blackness:

> While the tale of how we suffer, and how we are delighted, and how we may triumph is never new, it always must be heard. There isn't any other to tell, it's the only light we've got in all this darkness. . . . And this tale, according to that face, that body, those strong hands on those strings, has another aspect in every country, and a new depth in every generation. (*The Price of the Ticket*)

In this spirit, Ellis has declared the birth of a "New Black Aesthetic" movement, comprising artists and writers who are middle-class, self-confident, and secure with black culture, and not looking over their shoulders at white people, wondering whether or not the Mr. Wilsons of their world will call them George. Ellis sees creative artists such as Spike Lee, Wynton Marsalis, Anthony Davis, August Wilson, Warrington Hudlin, Joan Armatrading, and Lisa and Kelly Jones as representatives of a new generation who, commencing with the publication in 1978 of Toni Morrison's *Song of Solomon* (for Ellis, a founding gesture) "no longer need to deny or suppress any part of our complicated and sometimes contradictory cultural baggage to please either white people or black. The culturally mulatto *Cosby* girls are equally as black as a black teenage welfare mother" ("The New Black Aesthetic," *Before Columbus Review*, May 14, 1989). And Ellis is right: something quite new is afoot in African-American letters.

In a recent *New York Times Book Review* of Maxine Hong Kingston's new novel, Le Anne Schreiber remarks, "Wittman Ah Singh can't be Chinese even if he wants to be. . . . He is American, as American as Jack Kerouac or James Baldwin or Allen Ginsberg." I remember a time, not so very long ago, when almost no one would have thought of James Baldwin as typifying the "American." I think that even James Baldwin would have been surprised. Certainly since 1950, the meanings of blackness, as manifested in the literary tradition, have come full circle.

■ ■ ■

Consider the holy male trinity of the black tradition: Wright, Ellison, and Baldwin. For Richard Wright, "the color curtain" — as he titled a book on the Bandung Conference in 1955 when the "Third World" was born — was something to be rent asunder by something he vaguely called the "Enlightenment." (It never occurred to Wright, apparently, that the sublime gains in intellection in the Enlightenment took place simultaneously with the slave trade in African human beings, which generated an unprecedented degree of wealth and an unprecedentedly large leisure and intellectual class.) Wright was hardly sentimental about black Africa and the Third World: he actually told the first Conference of Negro-African Writers and Artists in Paris in 1956 that colonialism had been "liberating, since it smashed old traditions and destroyed old gods, freeing Africans from the 'rot' of their past," their "irrational past" (James Baldwin, *Nobody Knows My Name*). Despite the audacity of this claim, however, Wright saw himself as chosen "in some way to inject into the American consciousness" a cognizance of "other people's mores or national habits" ("I Choose Exile," unpublished essay). Wright claimed that he was "split": "I'm black. I'm a man of the West. . . . I see and understand the non- or anti-Western point of view." But, Wright confessed, "when I look out upon the vast stretches of this earth inhabited by brown, black and yellow men . . . my reactions and attitudes are those of the West" (*White Man, Listen!*). Wright never had clearer insight into himself, although his unrelentingly critical view of Third World cultures may make him a problematic figure among those of us bent upon decentering the canon.

James Baldwin, who in *Nobody Knows My Name*, parodied Wright's 1956 speech, concluded that "this was, perhaps, a tactless way of phrasing a debatable idea." Blackness, for Baldwin, was a sign, a sign that signified through the salvation of the "gospel impulse," as Craig Werner characterizes it, seen in his refusal "to create demons, to simplify the other in a way that would inevitably force him to simplify himself. . . . The gospel impulse — its refusal to accept oppositional thought; its complex sense of presence; its belief in salvation — sounds in Baldwin's voice no matter what his particular vocabulary at a particular moment" (Craig Werner, "James Baldwin: Politics and the Gospel Impulse," *New Politics* [Winter 1989]). Blackness, if it would be anything, stood as the saving grace of both white *and* black America.

Ralph Ellison, ever the trickster, felt it incumbent

upon him to show that blackness was a metaphor of the human condition, and yet to do so through a faithful adherence to its particularity. Nowhere is this idea rendered more brilliantly than in his sermon "The Blackness of Blackness," the tradition's classic critique of blackness as an essence:

"Brothers and sisters, my text this morning is the 'Blackness of Blackness.'"

And a congregation of voices answered: "That blackness is most black, brother, most black . . ."

"In the beginning . . ."

"At the very start," they cried.

". . . there was blackness . . ."

"Preach it . . ."

"and the sun . . ."

"The sun, Lawd . . ."

". . . was bloody red . . ."

"Red . . ."

"Now black is . . . " the preacher shouted.

"Bloody . . ."

"I said black is . . ."

"Preach it, brother . . ."

". . . an' black ain't . . ."

"Red, Lawd, red: He said it's red!"

"Amen, brother . . ."

"Black will git you . . ."

"Yes, it will . . ."

". . . an' black won't . . ."

"Naw, it won't!"

"It do . . ."

"It do, Lawd . . ."

". . . an' it don't."

"Hallelujah . . ."

"It'll put you, glory, glory, Oh my Lawd, in the WHALE'S BELLY."

"Preach it, dear brother . . ."

". . . an' make you tempt . . ."

"Good God a-mighty!"
"Old aunt Nelly!"
"Black will make you . . ."
"Black . . ."
". . . or black will un-make you."
"Ain't it the truth, Lawd?"   (*Invisible Man*)

Ellison parodies the idea that blackness can underwrite a metaphysics or even a negative theology, that it can exist outside and independent of its representation.

And it is out of this discursive melee that so much contemporary African-American literature has developed.

■ ■ ■

The range of representations of the meanings of blackness among the post–*Song of Solomon* (1978) era of black writing can be characterized—for the sake of convenience—by the works of C. Eric Lincoln (*The Avenue, Clayton City*); Trey Ellis's manifesto, "The New Black Aesthetic"; and Toni Morrison's *Beloved,* in many ways the Ur-text of the African-American experience.

Each of these writers epitomizes the points of a post–Black Aesthetic triangle, made up of the realistic representation of black vernacular culture: the attempt to preserve it for a younger generation (Lincoln), the critique through parody of the essentialism of the Black Aesthetic (Ellis), and the transcendence of the ultimate horror of the black past—slavery—through myth and the supernatural (Morrison).

The first chapter of Eric Lincoln's first novel, *The Avenue, Clayton City* (1988), contains an extended re-creation of the African-American ritual of signifying, which is also known as "talking that talk," "the dozens," "nasty talk," and so on. To render the dozens in such wonderful detail, of course, is a crucial manner of preserving it in the written cultural memory of African-

Americans. This important impulse to preserve (by recording) the vernacular links Lincoln's work directly to
that of Zora Neale Hurston. Following the depiction of
the ritual exchange, the narrator of the novel analyzes its
import in the following way:

> But it was playing the dozens that perplexed and worried
> Dr. Tait the most of all when he first tuned in on what went
> on under the streetlight. Surely it required the grossest level
> of depravity to indulge in such willful vulgarity. He had
> thought at first that Guts Gallimore's appraisal of talking
> that talk as "nasty" was too generous to be useful. . . . But
> the truth of the matter was that in spite of his disgust, the
> twin insights of agony and intellection had eventually paid
> off, for suddenly not only the language but the logic of the
> whole streetlight ritual finally became clear to him. What
> he was observing from the safety and the anonymity of his
> cloistered front porch was nothing less than a teenage rite of
> passage. A very critical *black* rite of passage! How could he
> not have recognized it for so long? The public deprecation of
> black men and women was, of course, taken for granted in
> Clayton City, and everywhere else within the experience of
> the Flame Gang. But when those black men and women
> were one's fathers, mothers, and sisters, how could one ap-
> proaching manhood accept that deprecation and live with
> it? To be a *man* implied responsibilities no colored man in
> Clayton City could meet, so the best way to deal with the
> contradiction was to deny it. Talkin' that talk — that is, dis-
> paraging one's loved ones within the in-group — was an obvi-
> ous expression of self-hatred, but it also undercut the white
> man's style of black denigration by presupposing it, and to
> some degree narcotizing the black boys who were on the way
> to manhood from the pain of their impotence. After all, *they
> had said it first!* Playing the dozens, Tait reasoned, was an
> effort to prepare one to be able to "take it." Anyone who
> refused to play the dozens was unrealistic, for the dozens
> were a fact of life for every black man. They were implicit
> in the very structure of black-white relations, and if one
> didn't "play," he could "pat his foot" while the play went

on, over and around him. No one could exempt himself from the cultural vulgarity of black debasement, no matter how offensive it might be.

Trey Ellis, whose first novel, *Platitudes*, is a satire on contemporary black cultural politics, is an heir of Ishmael Reed, the tradition's great satirist. Ellis describes the relation of what he calls "The New Black Aesthetic" (NBA) to the black nationalism of the sixties, engaged as it is in the necessary task of critique and revision:

> Yet ironically, a telltale sign of the work of the NBA is our parodying of the black nationalist movement: Eddie Murphy, 26, and his old *Saturday Night Live* character, prison poet Tyrone Green, with his hilariously awful angry black poem, "Cill [sic] My Landlord," ("See his dog Do he bite?"); fellow Black Packer Keenan Wayans' upcoming blaxploitation parody *I'ma Get You Sucka!*; playwright George Wolfe, and his parodies of both "A Raisin in the Sun" and "For Colored Girls . . . " in his hit play "The Colored Museum" ("Enter Walter-Lee-Beau-Willie-Jones. . . . His brow is heavy from 300 years of oppression."); filmmaker Reginald Hudlin, 25, and his sacrilegious *Reggie's World of Soul* with its fake commercial for a back scratcher, spatula and toilet bowl brush all with black clenched fists for their handle ends; and Lisa Jones' character Clean Mama King who is available for both sit-ins and film walk-ons. There is now such a strong and vast body of great black work that the corny or mediocre doesn't need to be coddled. NBA artists aren't afraid to publicly flout the official, positivist black party line.

This generation, Ellis continues, cares less about what white people think than any other in the history of Africans in this country: "The New Black Aesthetic says you just have to *be* natural, you don't necessarily have to *wear* one."

Ellis dates the beginning of this cultural movement to

the publication of *Song of Solomon* in 1978. Morrison's blend of magical realism and African-American mythology proved compelling: this brilliantly rendered book was an overnight bestseller. Her greatest artistic achievement, however, and most controversial, is her most recent novel, *Beloved*, which won the 1988 Pulitzer Prize for Fiction.

In *Beloved*, Morrison has found a language that gives voice to the unspeakable horror and terror of the black past, our enslavement in the New World. Indeed, the novel is an allegorical representation of this very unspeakability. It is one of the few treatments of slavery that escapes the pitfalls of *kitsch*. Toni Morrison's genius is that she has found a language by which to thematize this very unspeakability of slavery:

> Everybody knew what she was called, but nobody knew her name. Disremembered and unaccounted for, she cannot be lost because no one is looking for her, and even if they were, how can they call her if they don't know her name? Although she has claim, she is not claimed. In the place where long grass opens, the girl who waited to be loved and cry shame erupts into her separate parts, to make it easy for the chewing laughter to swallow her all away.
>
> It was not a story to pass on.
>
> They forgot her like a bad dream. After they made up their tales, shaped and decorated them, those that saw her that day on the porch quickly and deliberately forgot her. It took longer for those who had spoken to her, lived with her, fallen in love with her, to forget, until they realized they couldn't remember or repeat a single thing she said, and began to believe that, other than what they themselves were thinking, she hadn't said anything at all. So, in the end, they forgot her too. Remembering seemed unwise. They never knew where or why she crouched, or whose was the underwater face she needed like that. Where the memory of the smile under her chin might have been and was not, a latch latched and lichen attached its apple-green bloom to the

metal. What made her think her fingernails could open locks the rain rained on?

It was not a story to pass on.

Only by stepping outside the limitations of realism and entering a realm of myth could Morrison, a century after its abolition, give a voice to the silence of enslavement.

For these writers, in their various ways, the challenge of the black creative intelligence is no longer to *posit* blackness, as it was in the Black Arts movement of the sixties, but to render it. Their goal seems to be to create a fiction *beyond* the color line, one that takes the blackness of the culture for granted, as a springboard to write about those human emotions that we share with everyone else, and that we have always shared with each other, when no white people are around. They seem intent, paradoxically, on escaping the very banality of blackness that we encountered in so much Black Arts poetry, by *assuming* it as a legitimate grounds for the creation of art.

■   ■   ■

To declare that race is a trope, however is not to deny its palpable force in the life of every African-American who tries to function every day in a still very racist America. In the face of Anthony Appiah's and my own critique of what we might think of as "black essentialism," Houston Baker demands that we remember what we might characterize as the "taxi fallacy."

Houston, Anthony, and I emerge from the splendid isolation of the Schomburg Library and stand together on the corner of 135th Street and Malcolm X Boulevard attempting to hail a taxi to return to the Yale Club. With the taxis shooting by us as if we did not exist, Anthony and I cry out in perplexity, "But sir, it's only a trope."

If only that's *all* it was.

My father, who recently enjoyed his seventy-sixth birthday, and I attended a basketball game at Duke this past winter. It wasn't just any game; it was "the" game with North Carolina, the ultimate rivalry in American basketball competition. At a crucial juncture of the game, one of the overly avid Duke fans bellowing in our section of the auditorium called J. R. Reid, the Carolina center, "rubber lips."

"Did you hear what he said?" I asked my father, who wears *two* hearing aids.

"I heard it. Ignore it, boy."

"I can't, Pop," I replied. Then, loud-talking all the way, I informed the crowd, while ostensibly talking only to my father, that we'd come too far to put up with shit like this, that Martin Luther King didn't die in vain, and we won't tolerate this kind of racism again, etc., etc., etc. Then I stood up and told the guy not to say those words ever again.

You could have cut the silence in our section of that auditorium with a knife. After a long silence, my Dad leaned over and whispered to me, "Nigger, is you *crazy?* We am in de Souf." We both burst into laughter.

Even in the South, though, the intrusion of race into our lives usually takes more benign forms. One day my wife and my father came to lunch at the National Humanities Center in Research Triangle Park, North Carolina. The following day, the only black member of the staff cornered me and said that the kitchen staff had a bet, and that I was the only person who could resolve it. Shoot, I said. "Okay," he said. "The bet is that your Daddy is Mediterranean — Greek or Eyetalian, and your wife is High Yellow." "No," I said, "it's the other way around: my dad is black; my wife is white."

"Oh, yeah," he said, after a long pause, looking at me through the eyes of the race when one of us is being "sadiddy," or telling some kind of racial lie. "You, know, *brother*," he said to me in a low but pointed whisper,

"we black people got ways to *tell* these things, you know."
Then he looked at me to see if I was ready to confess the
truth. Indeterminacy had come home to greet me.

■   ■   ■

What, finally, is the meaning of blackness for my generation of African-American scholars? I think many of us are
trying to work, rather self-consciously, within the tradition. It has taken white administrators far too long to
realize that the recruitment of black faculty members is
vastly easier at those institutions with the strongest black
studies departments, or at least with the strongest representation of other black faculty. Why? I think the reason
for this is that many of us wish to be a part of a community, of something "larger" than ourselves, escaping the
splendid isolation of our studies. What can be lonelier
than research, except perhaps the terror of the blank page
(or computer screen)? Few of us — and I mean *very few* —
wish to be the "only one" in town. I want my own children to grow up in the home of intellectuals, but with
black middle-class values as common to them as the air
they breathe. This I cannot achieve alone. I seek out,
eagerly, the company of other African-American academics who have paid their dues; who understand the
costs, and the pleasures, of achievement; who care about
"the race"; and who are determined to leave a legacy of
self-defense against racism in all of its pernicious forms.

Part of this effort to achieve a sense of community is
understanding that our generation of scholars is just an
extension of other generations, of "many thousands
gone." We are no smarter than they; we are just a bit
more fortunate, in some ways, the accident of birth enabling us to teach at "white" research institutions, when
two generations before we would have been teaching at
black schools, overworked and underfunded. Most of us
define ourselves as extensions of the tradition of scholar-

ship and academic excellence epitomized by figures such as J. Saunders Redding, John Hope Franklin, and St. Clair Drake, merely to list a few names. But how are we *different* from them?

A few months ago I heard Cornel West deliver a memorial lecture in honor of James Snead, a brilliant literary critic who died of cancer this past spring at the age of thirty-five. Snead graduated valedictorian of his class at Exeter, then summa cum laude at Yale. Fluent in German, he wrote his Scholar of the House "essay" on the uses of repetition in Thomas Mann and William Faulkner. (Actually, this "essay" amounted to some six hundred pages, and the appendices were written in German.) He was also a jazz pianist and composer and worked as an investment banker in West Germany, after he took the Ph.D. in English literature at the University of Cambridge. Snead was a remarkable man.

West, near the end of his memorial lecture, told his audience that he had been discussing Snead's life and times with St. Clair Drake, as Drake lay in bed in a hospital recovering from a mild stroke that he had experienced on a flight from San Francisco to Princeton, where Drake was to lecture. When West met the plane at the airport, he rushed Drake to the hospital, and sat with him through much of the weekend.

West told Drake how Snead was, yes, a solid race man, how he loved the tradition and wrote about it, but that his real goal was to redefine *American Studies* from the vantage point of African-American concepts and principles. For Snead, taking the black mountaintop was not enough; he wanted the entire mountain range. "There is much about Dr. Snead that I can understand," Drake told West. "But then again," he concluded, "there is something about his enterprise that is quite unlike ours." Our next move within the academy, our next gesture, is to redefine the whole, simultaneously institutionalizing African-American studies. The idea that African-American culture is exclusively a thing apart, separate from the whole, having no influence on the shape and shaping of American culture, is a racialist fiction. There can be no doubt that the successful attempts to "decenter" the canon stem in part from the impact that black studies programs have had upon traditional notions of the "teachable," upon what, properly, constitutes the universe of knowledge that the well-educated should know. For us, and for the students that we train, the complex meaning of blackness is a vision of America, a refracted image in the American looking-glass.

Snead's project, and Ellis's — the project of a new generation of writers and scholars — is about transcending the I-got-mine parochialism of a desperate era. It looks beyond that overworked master plot of victims and victimizers so carefully scripted in the cultural dominant, beyond the paranoid dream of cultural autarky, and beyond the seductive ensolacements of nationalism. Their story — and it is a new story — is about elective affinities, unburdened by an ideology of descent; it speaks of blackness without blood. And this *is* a story to pass on.

CHAPTER
9

The Big Picture

I was drinking my second cup of coffee, watching "Good Morning, America," and trying to ignore the phone, which was ringing off the hook. It was too early for that, too damn early.

Joan Lunden was introducing this morning's special guest, an incredibly rumpled-looking biblical scholar. The guy had just published a best-selling book claiming that *The Anxiety of Influence* was written by a woman. Not all of it, understand. Just the passages about Blake and gnosticism. The good parts, in other words.

I reached for the remote and switched the damn thing off. My third cup of coffee was cold and rancid, just the way I liked it. I was ready to face the world.

That's when the phone rang again.

"Slade," the voice said. "Ain't you up yet? We got a real delicate situation."

I yawned. "Who is this?"

"You know damn well who. And you know why I'm calling, so let's skip the song and dance. I'll be at Sarabeth's in an hour—that's Amsterdam and Eighty-sixth. Meet me there. We'll talk about it over eggs and gravlax."

It was Jason Epstein. And he was right, I did know why he was calling. Christ, the whole town was buzzing with rumors about some kind of trouble at the Library of America project. Jason was editorial director at Random House, but the Library of America series was one of his pet projects. It was meant to be the American answer to the French Pléiade editions. The major works of the major authors, all lined up in a row. Viking distributed it in North America; Vintage, the Random House imprint, was doing the trade paperback editions. And everything was going like clockwork. Until recently.

Jason and I went way back. We first crossed paths when he was a wet-behind-the-ears gumshoe at Pinkerton's. Then he fell in with a fast crowd and ended up working the wrong side of the street, starting Anchor Books and the *New York Review of Books* and a lot of other stuff I didn't like to think about. We didn't exactly travel in the same circles anymore. He was hanging out with the real wise guys — like John Gotti, Tony Gambino, and Murray Kempton.

As for me, I was just trying to get by. I'd hung out my shingle as a private dick, which I guess was better than the other way around. It meant spending a lot of time on the fire escape of the local Best Western with my Minolta Slim-Line, snapping 35mm pics of couples engaged in extramarital recreation. Maybe that kind of work should have been beneath me — after all, I was with OSS during World War II — but at least divorce lawyers paid up front, and these days, you had to take what you could get.

Understand, I wasn't proud. *Sleazy* wasn't a word in my vocabulary. Hell, I used to break legs for Meyer Lansky. But with this Library of America thing, I wasn't sure what I was getting myself into.

I was fifteen minutes late for the meeting with Jason, and he'd ordered for me already. A gravlax omelet. I hate gravlax. The whole raw fish concept bothers me. Understand, I'm the kinda guy asks for his sushi well done.

"They're trying to kill my baby," he said, real soft.

"What are you talking about?"

We were seated at a corner table, and Jason handed me a pamphlet. "Take it as background," he grunted.

The pamphlet was real flossy. Elegant Baskerville type, white on black, above a red, white, and blue stripe running across the middle. "The Library of America," I read.

All of Melville, all of Hawthorne, all of James, and Emerson, and Thoreau — these and the writings of other notable American novelists, historians, poets, philosophers, and essayists are, for the first time in our history, being published in a series of handsome and durable volumes. Publication of this series is supported by grants from the Ford Foundation and the National Endowment for the Humanities. Thanks to their generosity, America, like other nations, can offer every reader the collected works of its major authors in authoritative editions. The commitment to publish an authoritative version of an author's work assures the reader that only after thorough research and study is a text selected for this series. For each volume, a distinguished scholar has prepared a succinct chronology of the author's life and career, an essay on the choice of texts, and some necessary notes. Library of America editions will last for generations and withstand the wear of frequent use. Sewn bindings allow the books to open easily and lie flat. The page layout has been designed for readability has well as elegance. Published by Literary Classics of the United States.

Then, under the red, white, and blue stripe, there was the italicized legend: "The collected works of America's foremost authors in uniform hardcover editions."

I said, "Looks good. So what's the rumpus?"

"As you can see, we got a commitment to uphold.

And *somebody*'s trying to stop us. Somebody with other plans for this stuff. I need to know who."

I shrugged. "Could be the Franklin Library. The guys with the leather-bound books with the ribs on the spine and the gilt-edged paper and the signed limited editions of Herman Wouk. Make sense, wouldn't it?"

"Don't teach your grandfather how to suck eggs. It ain't the Franklin Library," Jason growled into his double cappuchino, and I saw the froth go flat before my eyes. Now that's power. "Slade, we're not cretins. That's the first thing we checked into."

"You thinking politicos maybe? The IRA, the PLO, the MLA?"

"None of them has the clout. Now listen, you want the case, or you wanna go on taking nudie pics for Marvin Mitchelson?"

I sighed wearily. "Lay it all out, Jason. I'll know if you're holding back." As he talked, I cut my gravlax omelet into little bits and spread them around the circumference of my plate. That way, it looked like I'd eaten most of it. It was a trick I picked up as a little kid.

Usually worked, too.

Jason's story was pretty murky, but what it came down to was this. The whole Library of America thing was predicated on the fact that the stuff would be pretty much in the public domain. No copyright. The stuff's out there, and you print it. Sure, in a few cases, you deal with a literary executor, but there never was any hassle.

Then things turned bad. Standard copyright clearance forms they filed with the Library of Congress were being returned with notes about some kind of publication restrictions. Seemed the Senate subcommittee on copyright and intellectual property had attached a rider to a bill about tobacco subsidies, and nobody noticed what it said until it was too late. Point of it was, a loophole made it possible to convert from public domain status back to copyright governance. And somebody had done just that. Some foundation called the American Institute for Developmental Standards — an obvious front, Jason figured — had grabbed up the rights to the writings of America's foremost authors. They'd cornered the market. Like what the Hunt brothers tried to do with silver in the commodities market. Except this time it worked.

The whole Library of America project had ground to a halt. Worse still, all available editions of the works were being impounded. Legally. And there was nothing anyone could do about it.

Jason said the senators were obviously bought off, the American Bookseller Association was asleep at the wheel, and a monumental scam had been pulled on the whole publishing industry. Not to mention the reading public. Somebody had made off with the rights to the canon of "notable" American literature. And we had to get it back. Whatever it cost.

"Remember, Sam," he said. "This isn't just about business. This is about literature."

"Yeah? That's what they all say."

"I'm serious, dammit," he said. "People like us are the last barricade, the last line of defense culture *has* against commerce, against the tyranny of the bottom line." He paused, then looked up at me, his face more haggard than I'd ever seen it. "I *have* to believe that. Do you understand?"

I patted my pockets for a cigarette lighter. "One more thing," I said. "Any little detail, even if it seems completely trivial to you, could be important. You sure you told me everything?"

"Everything," he said, frowning. "Absolutely."

"What about these distinguished scholars you got editing these authoritative editions? Think they'd know anything?"

"You know, there *is* one little detail I forgot," he

added soberly. "They found all forty-seven of them last week. With their throats cut."

I nodded slowly. "Probably a coincidence," I allowed. But like I said, sometimes the unlikeliest details turned out to be significant.

After the waiter left the check on the table, I stood up. "For old time's sakes, I'll look into it, Jason. That's all I can promise."

Jason gestured at my plate. "What's the matter," he said, "you're not eating?"

■ ■ ■

I'm the kind of guy who takes things one step at a time. The only real lead we had so far was the front organization, that American Institute for whatever the heck it was. Jason wrote it off as a dead end. I wasn't so sure. The problem would be locating them. Their lawyers couldn't find any paper trail. But old Slade could still show those shysters a trick or two. Back on West End Avenue, I lay back on my green Naugahyde recliner, put my feet up, and tried to sort things out.

I settled on Slade's Rule Number Two: When in doubt, let your fingers do the walking. I took out the Manhattan phone directory and found what I was looking for in the white pages. The American Institute for Developmental Standards, 201 Madison Avenue. The listing was even in bold, and I know for a fact that costs an extra hundred bucks a year.

Street smarts, see. That's what they pay me for.

Two-oh-one Madison Avenue had a swank lobby with faux marble interiors and faux Aubusson carpeting. Only the closed-circuit video camera was for real.

I walked up to the building receptionist, a woman with frosted hair and a frostier attitude.

"I'm looking for the American Institute."

"You found it."

"You mean, this is it? The whole building?"

She nodded, then went back to her filing. The kind of filing you do with an emery board.

"Who's in charge here?"

"I just bet you'd like to know." She smiled. It was a nice smile, except her front teeth were smeared with lipstick.

I grabbed hold of her pearl choker and pulled her face close to mine. Real close. "No games. Who put you up to this?"

"Kelly Services," she said. "And it's my first day on the job. So gimme a break, OK?"

She was a hard case, obviously a seasoned professional, and I knew I wasn't going to crack her. I bounded up the curving stairway behind her teak-veneered workstation.

"Wait," she said. "You can't go up there." Then she went back to her emery board.

The second floor wasn't posh like the entrance. The floors were covered with industrial gray carpeting; the doors were metal, painted the greenish color of tarnished bronze.

All locked.

At the far end of the corridor, I spotted a man ducking around the corner. It was for just a split second, but I recognized him all the same. A guy who used to teach Expos 17 at Harvard before he was sacked. What was he doing here?

I loped after him, but I couldn't figure out where he'd gone. I couldn't see any other doors, just a phone booth at the end of the hallway. Then it dawned on me: the old phone booth trick. I walked into it, closed the door behind me, and the floor beneath my feet rotated soundlessly. Very state-of-the-art.

When I opened the door again, I found myself in a room the size of a gymnasium filled with a warren of cubicles, the kind made out of those movable half-height wall partitions. As best I could make out, the place housed a few hundred people, each seated in front of a computer terminal, typing away furiously. For the most part, they had the unmistakable look of the untenured collegian. Something stank. I could tell it was a sweatshop of some kind — but not like any I'd ever seen before.

My friend from Expos 17 was scurrying into a carrel nearby, and I caught up with him there.

Next to his computer monitor, an old book with cracked leather binding lay open, its pages beginning to yellow. I picked it up and took a look. It was Dreiser's *Sister Carrie*. The guy jerked like a startled rabbit and peered up at me.

"Mind telling me what the heck's going on?" I asked him conversationally.

"Get out of here, Slade," he said in a whisper just harsh enough to be heard over the hundreds of crackling keyboards. I could see the fear in his eyes — and the dark rings under them. He wasn't joking. "Get out of here if you know what's good for you."

But it was too late for that.

"Hey you!" somebody bellowed. "What are you doing here?" A burly man in an olive drab uniform and a crew cut was trotting toward me. I heard some frantic noise from his walkie-talkie and turned around, looking for a route of escape. Three grim-faced men wearing the same uniform strode toward me from different directions, looking like they meant business. They were the kind of guys who read *Soldier of Fortune*, not the *Antaeus Review*.

"Would you believe I got lost on my way to Oxford University Press?" I said to one of them, thinking fast. Then I felt a blow to the back of my head, and then the lights went out, and then I didn't feel anything at all.

■ ■ ■

When I came to, I was lolling around in the back of a limousine. My tongue felt furry, and the light hurt my eyes.

"I have a feeling," I mumbled, "we're not in Kansas anymore."

"Atlanta, Georgia, sir," the driver responded crisply without turning around. "On the way to the tower. Personal instructions from Mr. Turner."

I groaned.

"May as well enjoy it, sir," he said. He looked like one of those nice young men who pass around the plate for television evangelists.

He had a point. I rolled down a window. It was one of those balmy Atlanta days. The sun was warm, the breeze was gentle, and the air smelled faintly of peach blossoms. It reminded me why I lived in New York. I could never take exposure to the elements.

At the lobby of the Turner Communications Tower, another young man dressed in muted plaid arrived as my escort. Both buttons on his jacket were buttoned. He was obviously packing.

"Shall I take you up to see him?"

"Why don't you surprise me," I said.

The elevator opened at the twentieth floor, and I was led to an office with curving floor-to-ceiling windows and a wrap-around view of the city below. Plush. Very plush.

And there he was, the man himself. I'd be putting you on if I didn't admit my heart skipped a beat.

Rangy and tanned, Ted Turner stepped around from his desk and shook my hand as if I were a long lost friend.

"Naturally, we've been expecting a visitor like you," he said. His blue eyes twinkled a little. "You have quite a reputation, Mr. Slade." On a large video projection screen behind him, Judy Garland was singing "Somewhere Over the Rainbow."

"Funny," I said. "But I could have sworn that when I was a kid, the Kansas scenes in the *Wizard of Oz* were in black and white."

"Oh, that." He shook his head. "Metro-Goldwyn-Mayer was obviously short of funds. They skimped on the color, did a half-assed job. Fortunately, it's nothing that can't be fixed. And that's what Ted Turner Communications is all about. Fixing things. Getting the job done right."

"Brings in a lot of moolah, too." I looked around, lit a Lucky Strike, and took a long drag.

"Mr. Slade, I know why you were sent. We're both professionals. All I'm asking you to do is keep an open mind. My people tell me you're a reasonable man. Once you see what we're about here, I think you may have second thoughts about the assignment."

"I'm all ears," I said.

Fortunately, he was all mouth.

I took a seat by his desk and let him tell his side of the story.

"Do you have any idea how ignorant our young people are of our national classics?" he wanted to know.

I looked him in the eye, and I could tell he was serious. "I guess I read the same stories about it in *USA Today* as everybody else."

"My people have been doing research, and the situation's even worse that you'd think. The level of ignorance is abysmal. Thomas Carlyle once wrote that 'the history of a nation's poetry is the essence of its history,' and I think that in a broad sense, that's the indispensable function of literature in this great country of ours. Literature, great literature, is one of our most valuable treasures, and the best of it is going unread by too many people. Do you follow me? I'm talking about *market penetration*. Oh, sure, there are a few islands of elite education. The point is, we are not reaching the *people*. In my personal opinion, it's reached the point of a national crisis. I've got the facts and figures right here."

"Sorry, pal," I said, "I've heard this spiel a thousand times. So what else is new?"

"Well, by golly, I've decided it's time to do something about it."

"Is that why you shut down the Library of America?"

Ted Turner snorted. "Naive and destined to failure. Those people are slaves of the status quo. They are *not* taking the problem seriously."

"And you've got a better idea?"

He grinned triumphantly. "Don't I always?"

"I guess that's a matter of opinion."

"The Library of America puts out all that la-di-da about 'authoritative versions' of the author's work—I mean, honestly, they can stuff it. The main thing is to respect the original artistic integrity of a work—without being fanatical about it. See what I'm getting at? Name a book that every American ought to know."

I looked blank. It had been so many years. "I don't know—that Mark Twain book, *The Adventures of Huckleberry Finn.*"

"As a matter of fact, we're working on the revised standard edition at this very minute. And I'm very pleased with what we've done so far."

"You been making changes." So that's what was going on at 201 Madison Ave.

"Small improvements, not so anyone would notice, but let's face it, the book needs a little updating. We want a clean, wholesome product for a new America. The way it is—and I'm not denying it's a terrific book—but it's way too controversial, racially, if you see what I mean. And any whiff of that kind of thing can lead to loss of sales. Teachers don't teach the book because of perfectly understandable sensitivities, which means it's not assigned, which means unsold copies. Yet, while totally respecting the integrity of the original work, we can improve it in subtle but significant ways. That's why we hired Dr. Alvin Poussaint, the image consultant for the 'Cosby Show,' to supervise the revision. He's had *lots* of terrific ideas. The first few chapters just came back from rewrite this morning. Take a look for yourself."

I wasn't any kind of scholar, but even I could see the difference. No more darky dialect. I scanned a few more pages before looking up. "Maybe I'm slow, but haven't you gone a little overboard?"

"How do you mean?"

"It's one thing to clean up Jim's pronunciation, but here you've got him quoting—Friedrich Schleiermacher and teaching Huck about the concept of the sublime. A little out of character, ain't it?"

Turner looked mildly puzzled. "Well, but of course, Jim has a Ph.D. now. Makes him a much better role model, there being so few African-Americans with Ph.D.'s these days. On the revised storyboard, Jim earns a doctorate from the University of Heidelberg before he's accidentally sold into slavery. We're still respecting the integrity of Twain's artistic vision, mind you. The idea that Huck learns from Jim has always been a key theme in the book, most all the critics agree."

"Yeah, but—"

"So we've pushed that concept a little. Believe me, it's all in period. We've been incredibly scrupulous about that. Even brought in Hans Aarsleff to consult. But hey, that's really incidental to the plot. Basically, I envision this book as a cross between *Mississippi Burning* and *Steel Magnolias*. And we've already got an endorsement from Benjamin Hooks of the NAACP." He patted me on the shoulder. "You've got to hand it to me. A better literature, for a better America. Now that's *our* slogan."

"I suppose it'd be too much to hope that this ends with Sam Clemens."

"Shall we talk about *Moby Dick?*" Turner pulled out a glossy folder from his desk drawer. "Here's the marketing plan," he said. "Take a gander."

I looked through the proposal for a few minutes. Finally I asked him, "You really think this could work?"

Turner buzzed his secretary. "Barbara, what are the box office figures on *Red October?*"

A few moments later she reported in. "Eighty-five million dollars so far," she said. "That's not counting foreign rentals."

He looked at me and nodded. "I rest my case. Underwater plays. Tight spaces and constant danger. Melville understood that." He laid his hands flat on his desk and leaned forward: "I know, Melville lived before the age of audience testing, marketing analysis, zip-code targeting, and the like. He didn't need that stuff. See, he was a genius—had an intuitive sense of what would play."

I raised an eyebrow. "But these changes you're talking about—"

"I love Melville—it's quality material, and if there's one thing I respect it's quality. That doesn't mean he couldn't stand to be updated. Lose a little excess blubber, pardon the pun. The point is, *Moby*'s gonna be on wire racks in every drugstore in the country. Right next to the Tic Tacs and the Dentyne and the Mars Bars. Like I said—like everybody's been saying—people don't read literature anymore. Well, dammit, I'm doing something about it."

I cleared my throat quietly. "Some people—I'm saying *some* people—might look, um, askance at the giveaway prizes . . . like the gold-foil-wrapped chocolate doubloons that come free with each copy of *Moby*."

He chuckled. "Thought up that one myself. There's a little kid in everybody. I didn't learn that from transactional analysis; I learned it from marketing. But who's it hurt?"

"And then setting it all in a nuclear submarine. How's that going to go down?"

"Frankly, I doubt many people will even notice the change."

"And you really see mass market potential?"

"Absolutely. I'm teaming up with Chris Whittle for the publishing side, and he knows that market like the back of his hand."

"Whittle? That the fellow who publishes the books with ads in them?"

"It's the best way. Get 'em coming and going. He's already signed up sponsors for every classic of American literature."

"You mean, like *Billy Budd*'s going to have recruitment ads for the navy?"

He winced. "That was a tricky one. Apparently some people found certain veiled themes that worried this particular sponsor. Slight redraft, very slight. We decided to make sure that Starry Vere takes his wife on board. Claggart, too. That way, everyone can rest easy."

"I'm beginning to see how you think," I said. It made my skin crawl, but I decided to play it out. Blew a smoke ring in his direction and shook my head. "Somehow I don't think Henry James would appreciate that sort of marketing approach."

Ted clasped his hands together. "James," he said, "Now you're talking about someone close to my own heart. James had class, and you have to respect that— absolutely. I don't think anybody ever read him, but you knew it was classy stuff. And that's an image that we want to cultivate. We're talking *lifestyle*. You've got to be able to see yourself relaxing in an English men's club, the Athenaeum, say, seated in a tufted leather wing chair, smoking a old briar, sipping a fine Bas Armagnac, English Setter at your feet. You know, the whole Ralph Lauren thing."

Turner's eyes were bright. The guy obviously thought he was a visionary.

"That's why I'm building an imprint around him. Call it Preppy Lit. Classy Classics. Whatever. A little Edith Wharton, some Henry James, guys and gals who really knew how to live. And are willing, even eager to share it with you. We'll get Bruce Weber to do the cover shots just like he did for Ralph Lauren. Take Wharton's *Age of Innocence* — a lot of businessmen would look at it and see another nineteenth-century doorstop. I look at it and see *Bonfire of the Vanities* with petticoats."

I stubbed out my cigarette absently, didn't speak for a while. The whole thing made a scary sort of sense now.

"You're going to colorize the Library of America," I said.

He patted my cheek gently. "You got it."

I just sat there, trying to take it all in, trying to stay cool. Finally, I said, "So were do you go from here?"

"Accessories is the name of the game. You gotta accessorize. For starters, what do you think about Henry James as a line of clothing? I've asked Karl Lagerfeldt to look into it. But just imagine it. Jamesian jeans or houndstooth jackets — available exclusively at Bergdorf Goodman. We run these ads, see, with thirty-second skits based on the novels, and all the actors are modeling the collection, they're wearing Jamesian ties, Jamesian trousers, Jamesian jackets, the whole Jamesian wardrobe line. Those Eton shirts with the round collars. Plus we've entered into a joint product development plan with Caswell-Massey for Henry James, the cologne. We were going to have John Houseman play Henry in the ads, but when he kicked it, we decided to go for George Plimpton instead. We signed up Ivory and Merchant to produce and direct. The point is, you're not just trying to move *Roderick Hudson* or *The Golden Bowl* anymore. What you're selling is lifestyle. The sizzle, not the steak."

When Turner explained about his plans to turn the whole thing into a library of TV miniseries, I couldn't say I was surprised. I mean, I could see where he was coming from. He wasn't sticking with America, either. The library of world masterpieces was his purview. But when he mentioned Proust, I couldn't keep quiet anymore.

I looked at him hard. Real hard. "Marcel Proust?"

"Let you in on a secret: we're looking at Macaulay Culkin for the miniseries. Very up-close and personal. And the numbers are through the roof for the under-twelve crowd."

"*Death in Venice?*"

"Right now it's in turn-around. We're seeing a real heightened concern about child molesting these days, which could be a plus or a minus for the Nielsen ratings, depending how it plays. Other thing is, audience testing shows that Venice isn't a turn-on, so we're thinking maybe Venice, California."

"What about *Pamela?* Wait, don't tell me — Gloria Steinem was concerned about the treatment of women's empowerment."

"Not anymore." Turner looked pleased with himself. "God, the scene where she whips out the can of mace and says, 'Keep thy hands to thyself, or I shall blind thee like the burrowing mole thou art' — I mean, she's really taking control of the situation, for the first time in history. Bob Fisk — the guy who did the screenplay for *Lipstick*, with the Hemingway sisters? We put him in charge of the rewrite."

I swallowed hard. "*The Scarlet Letter?*"

"I like the letter concept, and I like the color. But there's no reason to be stuck with that *particular* letter. My thinking is, the letter *A*'s been — overexposed, I mean, being first and all. Not only that, but our general sense is, adultery just doesn't do it anymore. Basically, Dimmesdale is having a hard time getting in touch with his feelings, and Hester helps him to do that. Simple yet effective."

I felt the bile rising in my throat but I kept on. I had to know the worst. *"Daisy Miller?"*

"Like I told the boys today, it's perfect how it is, perfect—only, do it like *Dirty Dancing*. Best of all, though—we've already signed up Madonna to play Daisy. She's gonna throw in a few musical numbers, there'll be MTV spin-offs, I'm talking an audience share that will blow your mind."

"Bet it would," I said, poker-faced. I patted my pockets for my cigarette lighter again. Didn't feel it, but I felt something else. Seemed Turner's boys weren't such pros, after all.

I stood up slowly, glanced over Turner's shoulder at the flickering projection screen. Burt Lahr was telling Judy Garland, "Of *course* we believe ya', Dorothy."

But he didn't really. Dorothy was back in bed, in her little house in Kansas, and her bedspread was incredibly vivid in technicolor. That decided me.

"I find your plans extremely interesting, Mr. Turner," I said.

"There's lots more we haven't even gone into," he said.

"That won't be necessary." I reached into the deep breast pocket of my blue blazer and pulled out my trusty .32 Beretta. It was small, but like *Cosmo* always said, size wasn't everything.

I watched the color drain from Turner's face.

"You're a powerful man, Mr. Turner. Maybe even a visionary. It's not my job to say. But you're only flesh and blood. You put your pants on one leg at a time, just like everybody else. Oh sure, you're probably one of the

few people who could pull off something like this. Maybe
the only one. But remember, this gun is pointed right at
your heart."

"'That is my least vulnerable part.' Claude Raines in
Casablanca—we colorized it, you know."

"Sorry, but I'm a professional with a job to do, and I
will do whatever has to be done in order to stop you."
My voice was dead level, toneless, just the way I'd re-
hearsed it some nights when I was alone in my apartment. "Turner Communications may survive a lot of
things," I said, my fingers caressing the cool gun metal.
"But it won't survive Ted Turner."

That's when I heard a gravelly voice close behind me:
"Drop it, Sam."

I turned around slowly. It was Jason.

"Not you," I breathed. "Not you."

"Meet my new business partner," Turner said levelly.

"I can't believe it," I exploded. "After all you said
about commerce corrupting culture—"

Jason looked a little sheepish. "Hey, listen, Slade. The
guy can be awfully persuasive. I mean, he has a point.
And once he sat me down and explained things, well, it
seemed we had a lot in common. I never thought I'd
be saying this, but my eyes have been opened. Sure, his
approach took some getting used to, but now I truly believe it's the best way."

I looked skeptical—and probably mad as hell, to
boot.

"Dammit, Sam. It's the *only* way."

I put the Berreta down on Turner's desk.

"Don't be modest Jason," Turner said, putting an arm
around him. "Jason's going to be *very* useful to me. To
all of us. Tell him, Jason."

"Well, Ted decided there was no reason to stick with
the public domain stuff. We're gonna move into the
twentieth century, modern lit. He knows I can be useful

to him there, and frankly he's right. Of course, there are
a few holdouts. Ted's got a terrific rewrite of both *Herzog*
and *Mr. Sammler's Planet*, for instance."

Turner said, "Which is where we figure you could
come in handy, Slade. We need somebody like you.
Somebody who can deal with problem cases. Like for
starters, we've been finding Saul Bellow a rather difficult
man to deal with."

I nodded gravely. I knew which side my bread was
buttered on. More than that, I knew who owned the
butter in this town.

■ ■ ■

High over Los Angeles, making our final descent to LAX
in Ted Turner's private Boeing 707, Jason and Ted spoke
animatedly about production deals. They were headed
for a power lunch with Mike Ovitz at Spago. Meantime
Jane Fonda, dressed in a spandex suit, told me how much
she looked forward to playing Princess Cassimassima,
even as she did her leg lifts with metronomic regularity.
It wore me out just watching her.

"Jane," I told her from the bottom of my heart, "you
never cease to amaze me."

The flight attendant brought more champagne every
time my glass was empty, and I spent the flight thinking
over my own career decision. Mr. Turner knew what he
was up to, all right. And while I still didn't understand
why Emerson's *Journals* had to end with a high-speed
chase through the back streets of Marseille involving three
all-terrain vehicles and a stash of plastic explosives, who
was I to quibble? I didn't have the big picture.

And nobody was paying me to think, either. Jason
and Ted would take care of the literary classics of
America, and I waved good-bye as they disembarked. As
for me, my instructions were clear. It was off to Chicago
and the Committee on Social Thought. Time to break
some kneecaps.

10

Trading on the Margin: Notes on the Culture of Criticism

> "We must remember that until very recently Nigeria *was* British," said Miss Spurgeon. "It was pink on the map. In some old atlases it still is." Letty felt that with the way things were going, nothing was pink on the map any more.
> — BARBARA PYM, *Quartet in Autumn*

I

I recently asked the dean of a prestigious liberal arts college if he thought that his school would ever have, as Berkeley has, a majority nonwhite enrollment. "Never," he replied candidly. "That would completely alter our identity as a center of the liberal arts."

The assumption that there is a deep connection between the shape of a college curriculum and the ethnic composition of its students reflects a disquieting trend in American education. Political representation has been

173

confused with the "representation" of various ethnic identities in the curriculum, while debates about the nature of the humanities and core curricula have become marionette theaters for larger political concerns.

The cultural right, threatened both by these demographic shifts and by the demand for curricular change, has retreated to a stance of intellectual protectionism, arguing for a great and inviolable "Western tradition" which contains the seeds, fruit, and flowers of the very best that has been thought or uttered in human history, while the cultural left demands changes to accord with population shifts in gender and ethnicity (along the way often providing searching indictments of the sexism and racism that have plagued Western culture, and to which the cultural right sometimes turns a blind eye). Both, it seems to me, are wrongheaded.

As a humanist, I am just as concerned that so many of my colleagues, on the one hand, feel that the prime motivation for a diverse curriculum is these population shifts, as I am that those opposing diversity see it as foreclosing the possibility of a shared "American" identity. Both sides quickly resort to a grandly communitarian rhetoric. Both think they're struggling for the very soul of America. But if academic politics quickly becomes a *bellum omnium contra omnes*, perhaps it's time to wish a *pax* on both their houses.

What is multiculturalism, and why are they saying such terrible things about it? We've been told it threatens to fragment American culture into a warren of ethnic enclaves, each separate and inviolate. We've been told that it menaces the Western tradition of literature and the arts. We've been told it aims to politicize the school curriculum, replacing honest historical scholarship with a "feel good" syllabus designed solely to bolster the self-esteem of minorities. The alarm has been sounded, and many scholars and educators—liberals as well as conservatives—have responded to it. After all, if multicultur-alism is just a pretty name for ethnic chauvinism, who needs it?

There is, of course, a liberal rejoinder to these con-cerns, which says that this isn't what multiculturalism is—or at least not what it ought to be. The liberal plural-ist insists that the debate has been miscast from the begin-ning and that it is worth setting the main issues straight.

There's no denying that the multicultural initiative arose, in part, because of the fragmentation of American society by ethnicity, class, and gender. To make it the culprit for this fragmentation is to mistake effect for cause. Mayor Dinkins's metaphor about New York as a "gorgeous mosaic" is catchy but unhelpful, if it means that each culture is fixed in place and separated by grout. Perhaps we should try to think of American culture as a conversation among different voices—even if it's a con-versation that some of us weren't able to join until re-cently. Perhaps we should think about education, as the conservative philosopher Michael Oakeshott proposed, as "an invitation into the art of this conversation in which we learn to recognize the voices," each conditioned, as he says, by a different perception of the world. Common sense says that you don't bracket 90 percent of the world's cultural heritage if you really want to learn about the world.

To insist that we "master our own culture" before learning others only defers the vexed question: What gets to count as "our" culture? What makes knowledge worth knowing? Unfortunately, as history has taught us, an Anglo-American regional culture has too often masked itself as universal, passing itself off as our "common culture," and depicting different cultural traditions as "tribal" or "parochial." So it's only when we're free to explore the complexities of our hyphenated American cul-ture that we can discover what a genuinely common

American culture might actually look like. Common sense (Gramscian or otherwise) reminds us that we're *all* ethnics, and the challenge of transcending ethnic chauvinism is one we all face.

Granted, multiculturalism is no magic panacea for our social ills. We're worried when Johnny can't read. We're worried when Johnny can't add. But shouldn't we be worried, too, when Johnny tramples gravestones in a Jewish cemetery or scrawls racial epithets on a dormitory wall? It's a fact about this country that we've entrusted our schools with the fashioning and refashioning of a democratic polity; that's why the schooling of America has always been a matter of political judgment. But in America, a nation that has theorized itself as plural from its inception, our schools have a very special task.

The society we have made simply won't survive without the values of tolerance. And cultural tolerance comes to nothing without cultural understanding. In short, the challenge facing America in the next century will be the shaping, at long last, of a truly common public culture, one responsive to the long-silenced cultures of color. If we relinquish the ideal of America as a plural nation, we've abandoned the very experiment that America represents.

II

Or so argues the liberal pluralist. But it's a position that infuriates the hard left as much as the conservative rhetoric of exclusion distresses the liberal pluralist. The Conservative (these are caricatures, and I apologize), extolling the achievement of something narrativized under the rubric "Western civilization," says: Nobody does it better. We Liberal Reformists say: Do unto others as you would have them do unto you; and — hope for the best. The Left says: Let's do unto you what you *did* unto Others; and then see how you like that.

For them, what's distasteful about the ideology of pluralism is that it disguises real power relations; that it leaves the concept of hegemony unnamed; that it is a defeat that masquerades as victory; that it is an idyllic picture of coexistence that supervenes upon harsh realities. Pluralism, for them, fails to be adequately emancipatory; it leaves oppressive structures intact.

There are at least two things to notice here. First, if the hard left is correct, then the hard right has nothing to worry about from the multicultural initiative. Second, the hard left distinguishes itself from the liberal pluralist position in its frank partisanship; it subsists on a division between hegemons and hegemonized, center and margin, oppressor and oppressed, and makes no bones about which side it's on.

Finally, there is something more puzzling than it first appears about the more general objective: the redistribution of cultural capital, to use the term made familiar by Pierre Bourdieu. I think it's clarifying to cast the debate in these terms, and faithful to what's at the core of these recent arguments; I also think there's a reason that participants in the debate have been reluctant to do so. Again, let me enumerate.

First, the concept of *cultural capital* makes an otherwise high-minded and high-toned debate sound a little — sordid. The very model of cultural capital — by which the possession of cultural knowledge is systematically related to social stratification — is usually "unmasked" as an insidious mechanism; it's held to be the bad faith that hovers over the "liberal arts." You don't want to dive into this cesspool and say, I want a piece of it, too.

Second, a redistributionist agenda may not even be intelligible with respect to cultural capital. Cultural capital refers us to a system of differentiation; on this model, once cultural knowledge is redistributed so that it fails to mark a distinction, it loses its value. To borrow someone else's revision of Benjamin, this may be the work of reproduction in an age of mechanical art. We've heard, in this context, the phrase "cultural equity," a concept that may well have strategic value, but that is hard to make sense of otherwise, save as an illicit personification (the transferral of equal standing from people to their products). What could confer "equity" on "culture"? The phrase assumes that works of culture can be measured on some scalar metric — and decreed, from some Archimedian vantage point, to be equal. The question is why anybody should care about "culture" of this sort, let alone fight for a claim upon its title.

Third, the question of value divides the left in two. On the one hand, the usual unself-conscious position is to speak in terms of immanently valuable texts that have been "undervalued" for extrinsic reasons. On the other hand, the more "theorized" position views the concept of *value* as essentially mystified. That position has shrewdly demonstrated our usual assumptions about *theories* of value are incoherent, unintelligible, or otherwise unfounded; the only error it made was to assume that our *practices* of evaluation should, or could, fall by the wayside as well, which is surely a non sequitur. Indeed, the minute the word "judgmental" became pejorative, we should have known we made a misstep. Which isn't for a moment to concede that anybody actually stopped judging. Literary evaluation merely ceased to be a professionally accredited act.

Finally, neither left nor right escapes the Dean's dilemma. In short, we remain mired in the representation quandary.

III

The interplay between the two senses of the word *representation* has, indeed, been foundational to the now rather depleted argument over the "canon." On the one hand, it has dawned on most of us that the grand canon—this fixed repository of valuable texts—never existed as such, which is why it was such a pushover. On the other hand, more scholars have come to see that the conflation of textual with political representation fueled a windily apocalyptic rhetoric that had nowhere to go when its putative demands were granted. (It tended to sponsor a naively reductionist mode of reading, as well: Alice Walker as the black Eternal Feminine on two legs.) As John Guillory, perhaps our most sophisticated scholar of canon formation, has remarked,

> this sense of representation, the representation of groups by texts, lies at a curious tangent to the concept of *political* representation, with which it seems perhaps to have been confused, a confusion which is the occasion of both the impasse of co-optation and the very cachet of the noncanonical, contingent as it is upon the delegitimation of the canon. . . . The work of recovery has for the most part been undertaken as though the field of writing were a *plenum*, textual repetition of social diversity. In fact, as is quite well known, strategies of exclusion are employed historically most effectively at the level of access to *literacy*.

But the tension between the two senses of *representation* isn't restricted to arguments about the canon; in the minority context, the same issues resurface as an issue about the "burdens of representation" of the black artist. If black authors are primarily entrusted with producing the proverbial "text of blackness," they become vulnerable to the charge of betrayal if they shirk their duty. (The reason that nobody reads Zora Neale Hurston's *Seraph on the Suwannee* isn't unrelated to the reason that everybody reads *Their Eyes Were Watching God*.) Isaac Julien and Kobena Mercer, the black British filmmaker and theorist, have focused on the tension "between representation as a practice of depicting and representation as a practice of delegation. Representational democracy, like the classic realist text, is premised on an implicitly mimetic theory of representation as correspondence with the 'real.'" (As one of a small number of black filmmakers, Julien has felt the pressure to be in some sense "representative," so that his theoretical objections have an additional polemical edge.)

And while most of us will accept the point, I think many of us haven't appreciated the significance of this breach when it comes to the highly mediated relation between critical debates and their supposed referents.

Indeed, with the celebrated turn to politics in literary studies in the past decade — the decade since I earned my Ph.D. — there's been a significant change in the register of reproach. Pick up any issue of *Modern Philology* in the 1950s, and turn to the reviews section. You'll find that in those days, one would typically chastise a study for unpardonable lapses in its citations, for failing to take full account of the insight yielded by other scholarship, and would judge the author to be a slipshod ignoramus. Today, for equivalently venial offenses, the errant scholar can be reproached as a collaborationist, accused of unwitting complicity with the ideologies and structures of oppression, of silencing the voice of the Other, of colluding with perpetrators of injustice: "Thus Heywood's study only reinstates and revalorizes the very specular ideologies it appears to resist. . . . " The culprit, some fresh-faced young academic from the Midwest, stands exposed for what she is, a collaborator and purveyor of repression, a woman who silences entire populations with a single paragraph, who, in view of fatal analytic conflations, has denied agency to all the wretched of the earth.

Politics never felt that good.

It's heady stuff. Critics can feel like the Sorcerer's Apprentice, unleashing elemental forces beyond their control. But we know, on some level, that it's mostly make-believe, that the brilliant Althusserian unmasking of the ideological apparatus of film editing you published in *October* won't even change the way Jon Peters or Mike Ovitz treats his secretary, let alone bring down the house of patriarchy.

I guess that's why these levels of criticism often get mixed up. I've seen readers' reports on journal manuscripts that say things like "Not only does so-and-so's paper perpetuate a logic internal to the existing racist, patriarchal order, but footnote seventeen gives page numbers to a different edition than is listed in the bibliography." Well, we can't have that, now can we?

The dilemmas of oppositional criticism haunt the fractured American academic community. The 1980s witnessed not only a resurgence of what I'll call the New Moralism, but the beginnings of its subsidence. And this, too, is very much bound up with the problematic of representation, so that the relation between the politics of theory and the politics of politics became a question to be indefinitely deferred or finessed.

Seventies-style Hermeneutics killed the author; eighties-style Politics brought her back. The seventies sponsored a hedonic vocabulary of "free-play," *jouissance*, the joys of indeterminacy. The eighties brought back a grim-faced insistence on the hidden moral stakes; new-historicist essays on the English Renaissance, for instance, always turned out to be about Indians and empire.

Oppositional criticism in the early seventies offered us a sort of "wacky packs" version of literary history as a procession no longer of laureled heads but of clay feet. Later critiques of the canon went on to dispute its patterns of inclusion and exclusion. And as John Guillory has also pointed out, the reason the debate over the canon entailed the resurrection of the author was simply that it required a representative of a social constituency: the debate over canon formation was concerned, in the first instance, with *authors*, not texts.

And we "minority" critics came to play a similar role in the marionette theater of the political that I referred to earlier. We shouldn't wonder at the accompanying acrimony. Edward Said has indicted what he describes as the "badgering, hectoring, authoritative tone" that persists in contemporary cultural studies, adding, "the great horror I think we should all feel is toward systematic or dogmatic orthodoxies of one sort or another that are paraded as the last word of high Theory still hot from the press." Is it merely the uncanny workings of the old "imitative fallacy" that account for the authoritarian tonalities of scholarship and professional intercourse, where issues of domination are foregrounded?

Again, I want to stress the way in which minority criticism can become a site for larger contestations. Robert Young, an editor of the *Oxford Literary Review*, ventured an intriguing proposition in a recent paper entitled "The Politics of 'The Politics of Literary Theory.'" He notes that literary Marxism in contemporary America (as opposed to in Britain) has "few links with the social sciences or with a political base in the public sphere. You can make almost any political claim you like: you know that there is no danger that it will ever have any political effect." "At the same time," he continues,

> the pressure of feminism, and more recently Black Studies, has meant that today the political cannot be ignored by anyone, and may be responsible for the white male retreat into Marxism. Marxism can compete with feminism and Black Studies insofar as it offers to return literary criticism to its traditional moral function, but can, more covertly, also act as a defense against them.

The elided social referent of struggle returns, but now it is merely a struggle for the moral high ground. And I think you could argue that this return to a gestural sort of politics reflects a moralizing strain in contemporary criticism that has lost faith in its epistemological claims. Today, pace Yeats, even the mediocre lack all conviction. If we can't tell you what's true and what's false—the thought goes—we'll at least tell you what's right and what's wrong. What's wrong? Racism, colonialism, oppression, cultural imperialism, patriarchy, epistemic violence . . .

So we lost facts, and we got back ethics: a trade-in, but not necessarily an upgrade.

IV

One problem is, as I've suggested, that the immediate concern of the "politics of interpretation" is generally the politics of interpreters. Another is that we tend to equivocate between, on the one hand, what a text *could* mean (the possibilities of its signification, the "modalities of the production of meaning," as de Man has it) and, on the other hand, what a text *does* mean (the issue of its actual political effectivity). Political criticism usually works by demonstrating the former and insinuating the latter. Now, the pleasurable political frisson comes from the latter, the question of reception and effects (as an old newsroom slogan has it, if it bleeds, it leads). But critics are reluctant to engage in actual sociology: it isn't what they were trained to do; it's not what they were raised to value. Still, as political critics, we usually *trade* on that ambiguity.

Let me give you an example of a now familiar version of such political reading. In the course of elaborating a theory of "corporate populism," a recent critical essay accused Spike Lee of being responsible, though perhaps indirectly, for the death of black youths. The chain of causality begins with Spike, who makes television commercials that promote Air Jordans; it ends with the devastated, crack-ridden inner city — and a black youth with a bullet through the brain, murdered for his sneakers. All because Spike said that he's gotta have it. You think Mars Blackmon is funny? Those commercials have a body count.

I want to insist that this was not an aberration, but a state-of-the-art critical essay — which represents the impasse we've reached in the American academy. This is how we've been taught to do cultural politics. You find the body; then you find a culprit. It's also where the critique of the commodity will lead you. It's an old phenomenon on both the right and the left — and certain kinds of Marxism can be very theological on this point: Commodification is like original sin, and any cultural form it touches is tainted. And, of course, these critiques are usually anchored to semiorganicist notions of authenticity.

The old leftist critique of the commodity has a usefully confining tendency: it sets up a cunning trap that practically guarantees that the marginalized cultures it glorifies will remain marginalized. They knew just how to keep us in our place. And the logic was breathtakingly simple: If you win, you lose.

And that's because it's just a fact about what we quaintly label the "current conjuncture" that if a cultural form reaches a substantial audience, it has entered the circuits of commodification. What Paul Gilroy (after Werner Sollors) calls "Populist Modernism" stays in good ideological odor so long as it doesn't get too popular. And one of the most important contributions of a younger breed of cultural theorists has been a critique of the old critique of the commodity form. Kobena Mercer, for example, explores ways in which commodity forms have been expressively manipulated by the marginalized, to explore and explode the ideology of the "natural" and counterpose an aesthetics of artifice.

I want to propose that it's worth distinguishing between morality and moralism; but I do so with trepidation. As Logan Pearsall Smith has observed, "That we should practise what we preach is generally admitted; but anyone who preaches what he and his hearers practise must incur the gravest moral disapprobation." At the same time, I worry that the critical hair shirt has become more of a fashion statement than a political one.

A friend of mine suggested that we institutionalize something that we already do implicitly at conferences on "minority discourse": award a prize at the end for the panelist, respondent, or contestant most oppressed; at the end of the year, we could have the "Oppression Emmy" Awards. For what became clear, by the end of the past decade, was that this establishment of what J. G. Melquior calls an "official marginality" meant that minority critics are accepted by the academy; but in return, they must accept a role already scripted for them. Once scorned, now exalted. You think of Sally Field's address to the Motion Picture Academy when she received her Oscar: "You like me! You really, really like me!" we authorized Others shriek into the microphone, exultation momentarily breaking our dour countenances. (We can, of course, be a little more self-conscious about it and acknowledge our problematic positionality: "You like me, you really, really like me—you racist patriarchal Eurotrash elitists!") But let's face it. It takes all the fun out of being oppositional when someone hands you a script and says, "Be oppositional, please—you look so cute when you're angry."

What feel-good moralism had to confront was the nature of commodified postmodern ethnicity—which we could describe as the Benneton's model: "All the colors of the world," none of the oppression. It was a seductive vision: cashmere instead of power relations.

And it *was* a change. Usually, the Third World presented itself to us as the page people turn when the *Time* magazine ad says you can help little Maria or you can turn the page. It was a tropological locale of suffering and destitution. Now little Maria's wearing a purple angora scarf and a black V-neck sweater, and the message is: You can have style like Maria here and shop at Benneton's—or don't you even care about ethnic harmony?

To be sure, the Bennetonization of culture was not without its ironies: in New York, as Pat Williams has pointed out, the shops may not buzz you in if you actually look like one of those "ethnic" models. But as the eighties came to a close, a nagging doubt began to surface: Was academic politics finally a high-brow version of what *Women's Wear Daily* would call the "style wars"? I think that too easily lets us off the hook of history; I want to talk about the ways we've been betrayed by our two-decades-long love affair with theory. Oscar Wilde once quipped that when good Americans die, they go to Paris. I think in Paris, when good theories die, they go to America.

In retrospect, it was easy to point to blunders, some of which I've mentioned. Righteous indignation became routinized, professionalized, and, in so doing, underwent an odd transformation. Back in the 1930s, a magazine editor wondered aloud if there was a typewriter at the *Partisan Review* with the word *alienation* on a single key. Right now I'm on the lookout for a typewriter that has *counterhegemonic cultural production* on a single key.

V

And one of the most interesting developments in the past decade took place when theoretically sophisticated minority scholarship parted company with its left-theoretic mentors. I want to take my example here not from literature, but from law, and the field of critical legal studies (CLS) in particular. The participants include Maria Matsudo, Richard Delgado, Patricia J. Williams, and the philosopher Cornel West, who was one of the only non-lawyers involved. What was revealed was a principled distrust for a radically utopian strain in CLS. West took to task American leftism for its undialectical, purely antagonistic relation to liberalism: If you don't build on liberalism, he argued, you build on air. In this vein, the minority legal scholars pointed out that those rudiments of legal liberalism — the doctrine of rights, for example, formality of rules and procedures, zones of privacy — that CLS wanted to trash as so much legalistic subterfuge were pretty much all they had going for them. So the irony was, when all the dust had cleared (I'm oversimplifying, of course, but not hugely), that the left minority scholars had retrieved and reconstituted liberalism. Some may well dismiss this as just another example of "uneven theoretical development," the minoritarian resistance to universalizing theory. It would be too easy thus to dismiss one of the most telling intellectual twists of recent memory.

And one that also points to the way in which critical theory had failed to keep pace with the larger world. The very notion of an ethical universal — for years dismissed as hopelessly naive — is beginning to make a comeback in the works of a number of feminist theorists. We had so much fun "deconstructing" the liberal ideology of "rights," for example, that we lost sight of how strategically — humanly — valuable the notion proved in, for example, much third world politics (as Abdullahi Ahmed An-Na'im, Francis Mading Deng, and others have shown).

Turning a baleful eye to its fellow disciplines, literary criticism has spent the last two decades singing: "Anything You Can Do, I Can Do Better"—rather like a scratched Ethel Merman recording. Which makes the difficulty literary critics have had in grasping-some elementary ideas rather poignant; what was once a resistance to theory has turned into a resistance to anything not packaged as theory.

The oppositional style of criticism has failed us, failed us in our attempt to come to grips with an America that can no longer be construed as an integral whole. What Richard Hofsteader famously called the "paranoid style" of American politics has become the paranoid style of American studies.

None of this is of recent vintage, of course. In 1930, Lionel Trilling could write, "There is only one way to accept America, and that is in hate; one must be close to one's land, passionately close in some way or other, and the only way to be close to America is to hate it. . . . There is no person in the United States, save he be a member of the plutocratic class . . . who is not tainted, a little or much, with the madness of the bottom dog, not one who is not in sympathy of disgust and hate with his fellows." For these are "the universally relevant emotions of America."

Today, success has spoiled us; the right has robbed us of our dyspepsia; and the routinized production of righteous indignation is allowed to substitute for critical rigor.

And nothing more clearly marks our failure to address the complexities of the larger world than the continuing ascendancy, in contemporary criticism, of what could be

called the colonial paradigm. Colonialism, more as metaphor than as a particularized historical phenomenon, has
proved astonishingly capacious; Fanon is blithely invoked
to describe the allegedly "colonizing" relation between
English departments and history departments. The irony
is that in the meantime, the tendency in subaltern studies
has been to pluralize the notion of "colonization," to insist
on the particularity of its instances, and to question the
explanatory value of the general rubric. So, too, with the
concept of "neocolonialism," which is increasingly re-
garded as both exculpatory of despotic third world regimes and, thirty years after independence, too vague to
be helpful in characterizing the peculiarities of these
states in the world economy.

There's a passage in one of Barbara Pym's late novels,
Quartet in Autumn, that comes to mind as a splendid
instance of colonial nostalgia (the novel is set in the mid-
seventies, I should mention). Letty, one of the principal
characters (all of whom are petty office workers on the
brink of retirement), is told that her landlord has sold the
house, and that a certain Jacob Olatunde, from Nigeria,
will be their new landlord. None of the tenants takes it
well — all will shortly relocate — but one tries to be philosophical about it:

> "We must remember that until very recently Nigeria *was*
> British," said Miss Spurgeon. "It was pink on the map. In
> some old atlases it still is."
> Letty felt that with the way things were going, nothing
> was pink on the map any more.

But the sovereign–colony relation is simply another
instance of the spatial topography of center and margin
on which oppositional criticism subsists. And it is just this
model that, I want to suggest, has started to exhaust its
usefulness in describing our own modernity.

VI

Let me say at once that I do not have in mind what some people have trumpeted as the new Pax Americana. In his recent "reflections on American equality and foreign liberations," David Brion Davis remarks, apropos of the recent decline of Eastern bloc communism, that "Nothing could be more fatuous than to interpret these developments . . . as a prelude to the Americanization of the world." He reminds us of Marx's view that capitalism itself is "permanently revolutionary, tearing down all obstacles that impede the development of productive forces, the expansion of needs, the diversity of production and the exploitation and exchange of natural and intellectual forces." But to view recent events as a triumph of American corporate capitalism, which has failed to abate the immiseration of the so-called underclass in its own backyard, is simply to misread history. (The Chinese students at Tianenman Square quoted Locke and Jefferson, not Ayn Rand or Lee Iaccocca.) At the same time, I think Davis establishes that the historiographical tradition that depicts America univocally as a force of reaction in a world of daisy-fresh revolutionary ferment reduces a history of complex ambivalence to a crude morality tale.

A great deal of weight has been assigned to the term *cultural imperialism:* I do not know that much time has been spent thinking about what the phrase should mean. Should the global circulation of American culture always be identified as imperialism, even if imperialism by other means? In an era of transnational capital, transnational labor, and transnational culture, how well is the center–periphery model holding up?

The distinguished anthropologist Arjun Appadurai has drawn our attention to that "uncanny Philippine affinity for American popular music." "An entire nation," he writes, "seems to have learned to mimic Kenny Rogers

and the Lennon sisters, like a vast Asian Motown chorus."
All this, in a former U.S. colony racked by enormous
contrasts of wealth and poverty, amounting to what he
describes as "nostalgia without memory." And yet the
usual remarks about "cultural imperialism" fail to acknowledge the specificity of cultural interactions. An
American-centered view of the world blinds us to the fact
that America isn't always on center stage, whether as
hero or as villain. As Appadurai writes:

> . . . it is worth noticing that for the people of Iran Jaya,
> Indonesianization may be more worrisome than American-
> ization, as Japanization may be for Koreans, Indianization
> for Sri Lankans, Vietnamization for the Cambodians, Rus-
> sianization for the people of Soviet Armenia and the Baltic
> Republics. Such a list of alternative fears to Americanization
> could be greatly expanded, but it is not a shapeless inventory:
> for the polities of smaller scale, there is always a fear of
> cultural absorption by polities of a larger scale, especially
> those that are nearby. One man's imagined community is
> another man's political prison.

What we are beginning to see, in work that proceeds
under the rubric of "public culture," is, as Appadurai
concludes, that "the new global cultural economy has
to be seen as a complex, overlapping, disjunctive order,
which cannot any longer be understood in terms of existing center-periphery models (even those which might
account for multiple centers and peripheries)." Again,
I want to suggest that the spatial dichotomies through
which our oppositional criticism has defined itself prove
increasingly inadequate to a cultural complex of traveling
culture. Once more, the world itself has outpaced our
academic discourse.

Melville's America retained a strong sense of its marginality vis-à-vis its former sovereign and colonizer. And
yet his assertion that we are "not a nation, so much as a

world" has *become* true, as a geopolitical fact. As a result, the disciplinary enclave of American studies is surely the proper site to begin a study of both the globalization of America and the Americanization of the globe—and, equally, the resistance bred by both of these trends. I think this is a project worth pursuing even if it does not come without a price. Surely it is clear to us all that the ritualized invocation of Otherness is losing its capacity to engender new forms of knowledge, that the "margin" may have exhausted its strategic value as a position from which to theorize the very antinomies that produced it as an object of study.

Or as Audre Lorde writes, in her poem "Good Mirrors Are Not Cheap":

> It is a waste of time hating a mirror
> or its reflection
> instead of stopping the hand
> that makes glass with distortions

But I've been misunderstood in the past, so I want to be very clear on one point. While I may be taken to have argued for the retrieval of liberalism, however refashioned, as a viable, reformable agenda, I distrust those— at the left, right, or center—who would erect an opposition between leftism and liberalism. Cornel West has rightly argued that a left politics that can imagine only an agonistic relation to real-world liberalism is a bankrupt politics; but the converse is true as well: A rights-based liberalism unresponsive to radical (and conservative) critiques is an impoverished one indeed. So let me make it clear that my remarks are aimed primarily at those massively totalizing theories that marginalize practical political action as a jejune indulgence. It's a critique I made a few years back about Irigiray—that her conception of the amazing fixity of patriarchy, the complete unavailability of any external purchase, is more likely to send us to the margins of Plato, Freud, and Lacan than to encourage anything so vulgar as overt political action. It's her embrace of systematicity — and this is something common to a certain structural-functional tradition of social thought, a tradition whose grand paranoias have made it particularly seductive to literary criticism — that rules out humble amelioration. And while some of the masters of grand total theory will concede the need to struggle for such unglamorous things as "equal wages and social rights," the fact that they feel obliged to make the (rather left-handed) concession indicates the difficulty; their Olympian, all-or-nothing perspective cannot but enervate and diminish the arena of real politics. In short, my brief — and that of many minority intellectuals to-day — is against the temptations of what I call Messianic pessimism.

Nor, however, can we be content with the multiplication of authorized subjectivities, symbolically rewarded by virtue of being materially deprived. Perhaps we can begin to forgo the pleasures of ethnicist affirmation and routinized resentment in favor of rethinking the larger structures that constrain and enable our agency. In an increasingly polycentric world, our task may be to prepare for a world in which nothing is pink on the map.

Index

African-American autobiographical moment (Baker), 40
African-American, birth of, 138–
39
African-American critic, task of,
36–42
African-American culture, xvii,
123–27
African-American literary tradition, 65, 75–76, 78, 79, 80
African-American literature, 30,
31, 88–103
African-American scholars/edu-
cators, 149
African-American Studies, xiii,
92, 93, 140–41, 143
African-American tradition,
canon formation and, 17–42,
51–55
African culture, 123, 142–43
Allen, William G., 25–26
American literature, canon of,
30, 39
, 40

Appadurai, Arjun, 190–91
Appiah, Kwame Anthony, 66–67,
68–69, 114, 147
Arts, equal access to, 122–23. *See
also* Black arts movement

Bacon, Sir Francis, 73, 108,
120; *The New Organon*, 57–
58
Baker, Houston A., Jr., 76, 77,
147. *See also* Fiedler, Leslie
Baldwin, James, 110, 139, 141;
Notes of a Native Son, 101
Bambara, Toni Cade, 91
Baraka, Amiri, 101; (and Larry
Neal) *Black Fire*, 30
Bennett, William, 17, 33
*Black American Literature Fo-
rum*, 81
Black arts movement, 93, 101–2,
147
Black Fire (Baraka and Neal),
30
Black mother, 40–41

"Blackness," 138, 140; for Baldwin, 141; for Ellison, 141–43; range of meanings of, 143–47, 149–51; text of, 179
Black Papers Projects, 122
Black Periodical Literature Project, 122
Black political signified, 82
Black studies. *See* African-American Studies
"Black Theory," 81
Bloom, Allan, xvi, 17, 36–37, 108, 118
Bosman, William, 59
Brooks, Gwendolyn, 91
Burch, Charles Eaton, 90

Calverton, V. F., 27, 28, 29; *An Anthology of American Negro Literature*, 26
Canon: of American literature, 30, 39; black, 24–25, 29, 39, 79, 97; formation, 17–42; Western, 33, 35
Casely-Hayford, J. E., *Ethiopia Unbound*, 76
College campuses, incidents of racial violence and racism on, 18, 105, 106, 135
College Language Association, 95
Colonial paradigm, 189
Commission on Minority Groups and the Study of Language and Literature (MLA), 95
Commodity, 56–62, 184
Commonplace book of shared culture, 21
Critical theory, 80, 187–88
Criticism: black, development of, 102–4; black, future of, 81; black, language of, 82–83; oppositional, 188, 191; political, 183

Critics: of Afro-American literature, 75–80, 83; minority, 182, 185. *See also* African-American critic; Criticism
Crummell, Alexander, 72–75, 83
Cugoano, Ottobah, 63
Cultural capital, 177–78
Cultural equity, 178
Cultural geneticism, 108–12
Cultural imperialism, 190–91
Cultural nationalism, xvi, 118
Cultural pluralism. *See* Multiculturalism; Pluralism
Cultural politics, 184
Cultural studies rubric of African-American Studies, 123
Culture: public, 47, 176, 191; pluralist view of, xv–xvi. *See also* African-American culture; Western culture
Curriculum, xiii; core, 42, 174

Davis, David Brion, 190
Delgado, Richard, 187
Derrida, Jacques, 35, 66, 67
Dewey, John, 119–20
Dismantlement, paradigm of, 37–38
Douglass, Frederick, 59
Dove, Rita, 91
Drake, St. Clair, 150
Du Bois, W.E.B., xii, 72, 83, 111–12, 122

Education: American, theories of, 106; broadening vistas of, 112–13; political nature of debate over, xiv; universal, justification for, 34
Ellison, Ralph, 91, 141–43
Ellis, Trey, 131, 139–40; "The New Black Aesthetic," 143, 145

Emerson, 22, 23, 24
English Institute, 95
Enlightenment, 54, 55, 57
Enrollment, black, 106–107
Equiano, Olaudah, 63
Ethnic studies departments, 117, 118

Feminism. *See* Women's movement
Fiedler, Leslie, (and Houston A. Baker, Jr.) *Opening Up the Canon: Selected Papers from the English Institute*, 95, 97–98
Fisher, Dexter: *Minority Language and Literature*, 95, 96; (and Robert Stepto) *Afro-American Literature: The Reconstruction of Instruction*, 95, 96–97

Great Chain of Being, 55, 56, 64–65
Gronniosaw, James, 63–64
Guillory, John, 179, 181
Gutmann, Amy, *Democratic Education*, 118

Hamilton, Charles V., *Encyclopedia of Black Culture*, 121
Harlem Renaissance, 27, 54
Hegel, G.W.F., 61, 73; *Philosophy of History*, 54
Herder, Johann, 24
Heylyn, Peter, *Little Description of the Great World*, 58
High schools, status of black literature in, 90–91
Hines, Darlene Clarke, 121
History, 19, 34–35, 61, 62
Hulme, William Henry, xiv
Humanities, 111; equal access to, 122–23; fragmenting versus decentering, 113–18; human notion of, 42, 118; nature of, 174
Humanity, 73; absence of, 57–62, 63
Hume, David, 54, 59, 64, 73, 78; "Of National Characters," 60
Hurston, Zora Neale, 144, 179
Hutchins, Robert Maynard, 119

Integrity, 77, 78

Jackson, Rebecca Cox, 67–68
Jaynes, Gerald. *See* Williams, Robin
Jea, John, 63
Jefferson, Thomas, 73; *Notes on the State of Virginia*, 61
Jeffries, Leonard, xvi
Johnson, James Weldon, 90; *The Book of American Negro Poetry*, 26–27
Julien, Isaac, 179

Kant, Immanuel, 54, 61, 63, 73; *Observations on the Feelings of the Beautiful and the Sublime*, 60–61
Kerner Commission Report (1968), 123, 137

Laforest, M. Edmond, 66
Language, 47, 49–51, 79
Lanusse, Armand, *Les Cenelles*, 24–25
Lee, Spike, 184
Liberalism, 187, 192
Lincoln, C. Eric, *The Avenue, Clayton City*, 143
Literacy, 58–59
Literary history, 34
Literary theory: redefinition of, 83; relation between literature and, 76–79

Literature: comparative, 118; import of race in study of, 44–48; minority, 95–96; relation between theory and, 76–77; teaching of, 35. *See also* African-American literature; American literature

Locke, Alain, *The New Negro*, 26

Marrant, John, 63
Matsudo, Maria, 187
Melville, Herman, 116, 191
Mercer, Kobena, 179, 184
Modern Language Association, 95
Morrison, Toni, 91, 92–93; *Beloved*, 143, 146–47; *Song of Solomon*, 140, 146
Multiculturalism, xi–xvii, 116, 117–18; debates about, xiii; description of, 174–76; origin of in Afro-American Studies, xiii; as representing the *mathesis universalis* ideal, xv

National spirit, reflection of in works of art, 45, 46–47
Naylor, Gloria, 91
Neal, Larry, 101; (and Amiri Baraka) *Black Fire*, 30
The Negro Caravan, 27, 28
"The New Black Aesthetic," 143, 143; movement, 103, 139–40
Newman, Cardinal, xv
Norton Anthology of African-American Literature, 31, 121

"Other," 45, 55, 59, 83, 110
Oxford Companion to African American Literature, 121
Ozick, Cynthia, 34

Pan-African ethnicity, 126
Parker, Theodore, 22–24
Pattee, Fred Lewis, xiv
Pennington, Reverend James W. C., 55, 59
Pluralism, xi, xii, xiii, 119–20, 176–77
Pluralists, view of culture of, xv, xvi
Politicization, of Western canon, 33
Politics: of interpretation, 183; turn toward in literary studies, 19, 180
"Populist Modernism," 184
Public policy rubric, of African-American Studies, 123–24

Race: according to Taine, 45–46; fiction of as meaningful criterion within biological sciences, 48–51; how writing relates to, 69; as a meaningful category in study of literature, 44–48; sense of difference defined in popular usages of, 49–51
Race, moment, and *milieu* (Taine), 45
Racial differences, 46, 69
Racism, 78, 147; on college campuses, 18, 105, 106, 135
Reason, writing as visible sign of, 54, 56, 57
Reed, Ishmael, 118, 145
Representation quandary, 178, 181

Said, Edward, xv, 182
Schomburg Library of 19th Century Black Women's Writings, 121
Self-identification, 36–37

Shange, Ntozake, *For Coloured Girls Who Have Considered Suicide*, 93
Signifying, 143
Slave narratives, 23, 57, 63–66
Smith, Logan Pearsall, 185
Snead, James, 150
Social construction, 37
Social reproduction, 106
Soyinka, Wole, 88, 126
Spillers, Hortence, 40–41
Stepan, Nancy, *The Idea of Race in Science*, 50
Stepto, Robert. *See* Fisher, Dexter
Subjectivity, attempts to reconstitute, 35–36
Sumner, Charles, 23–24

Taine, *History of English Literature*, 45–46
Talking book, 63, 64, 65
Tate, Greg, 80–81
Theory. *See* Literary theory
Third World, 140, 141

Universal knowledge, creed of, 108–9

Vernacular, black, 27–28, 33, 74, 83

Walker, Alice, 91, 92; *The Color Purple*, 68
Wallace, Michele, *Black Macho and the Myth of the Superwoman*, 93
West, Cornel, 150, 187, 192
Western culture, xvi, 33
Western literary tradition, 44
Western tradition, 68; hegemony of, 38
Wheatley, Phillis, 51–53, 61, 78; *Poems on Various Subjects, Religious and Moral*, 53
Williams, Robin, (and Gerald Jaynes) *A Common Destiny*, 121
Women's movement, within African-American literature, 91–93
World culture, preparation of students as citizens of, 42
World literature, 97–98
Wright, Richard, 103, 110–11, 140–41
Writing: according to Hume, 64; of Africans, and slavery debates, 54–55; Anglo-African, rise of, 62–63; black, 65–66; confinement and delimitation of black tradition by, 51–55; as medium of expression of reason, 56, 57; relationship of to humanity, 57–62, 63; relationship of to race, 69; transformation of from an activity of mind into a commodity, 56–62

Young, Robert, 182